the
BEKEN
file

the
BEKEN
file

by Keith Beken

Channel Press

Channel Press
In association with Ginn & Company Ltd
Elsinore House, Buckingham Street,
Aylesbury, Buckinghamshire HP20 2NQ, UK

First published as
Beken, Ma Vie
© Librairie Arthaud in Paris 1979

First published this edition 1980
ISBN 0 906781 02 7

Typographical design by Constance and Brian Dear
Typeset in Baskerville by Westholme Graphics, Cambridgeshire
Printed in England by Fakenham Press, Fakenham

Contents

Illustrations

. . . no cure for sea fever

Introduction

. . . It's blowing Force 5, gusting 6; white messengers are scudding low across the sky, foretelling storm; the sun is bright to the eye; we, in our cockleshell, are on an endless safari, sliding and pirouetting on the surfing waves in a perpetual ballet. In the distance, a flash of red rising and then dipping into the troughs between the rolling seas: approaching, we see an ocean racer with her huge red spinnaker bursting out to leeward—she takes a Force 6 gust, like the kick of a mule, and heels over, her ear to the sea. She rises, her spinnaker fills with the clap of thunder and she leaps toward us; in our tiny shell of a boat, we feel that we are at the end of our safari, with the rare 'white snow leopard' that we have been hunting all day now in our sights.

We edge near, our stern rises high and kicks spray at us as we slide into our target. Another gust hits the racer as she comes abeam and she shows the whole of her keel and rudder, exposed to the air—'Quick Ken, let's shoot her in her quarter'—we spin across her stern and note *Rendez-vous*—Malmo emblazoned on her transom. Lifted high above her deck, we see the helmsman struggling with his wheel; and then we are sucked surfing down into her quartering wave, in the lee of that towering mass of sail.

The seas snarl and growl along her deck, raising a plume of white water as they smash into the main boom end—again she takes a 'knock down', and we shoot her as she lies like a near-mortally wounded creature.

◄

Myth of Malham

Suddenly she rises and shakes herself, the water cascading off her deck and, as another great gust hits her, she rounds upon us in a furious turn. With spinnaker aback and mainsail thrashing, she charges us like some wild animal with foam flying from her mouth—we shoot and shoot again and then flee from her wrath; regaining her control, *Rendez-vous* turns away, her spinnaker fills, and she sails to join her friends. . . . We are content.

To those of you who have known and loved the sea—you will understand; to those of you who haven't even seen it, think of the part it plays in your lives. You wash in it, swim in it, even write songs about it. People sail around the world on it, and the fruits of the earth are carried to you upon it; the world in general and Eskimos in particular eat the fish from it. We read from the Bible that Someone walked upon it. Another person whom I know well also tried, after a 'liquid' evening ashore during Cowes Week— he succeeded only in losing his spectacles.

I'll try to convey to you the love and joy I myself have had from the sea. You can use it for nothing, sail at night, and watch the sunset turn from gold to blood . . . and later you will hear and see things that you have never experienced before—but meanwhile let us turn back to the days of fiddle, spoon and clipper bows, of ratlines and futtocks, of throats and peaks and masthoops, of polished brass and sweeping teak-laid decks: the good old days. . . .

Keith Beken.

The Good Old Days

The year is 1837. King William IV is dead, and the young Princess Victoria has become Queen of England. The Isle of Wight, and particularly Cowes at the mouth of the river Medina, had already been popular with the Princess—so much so that, when she became Queen, she decided to build a large house on the eastern side of the river; and 'Osborne House', as it was called, became her summer residence.

In the 1850's with the Royal Yacht *Alberta* moored in the Solent in full view of Osborne House, Cowes became a very fashionable watering place—a royal court, in fact—and it became the thing not only to own a yacht but to own one bigger and more luxurious than those of one's friends or competitors. So Cowes became the venue for visiting kings, queens and royalty from all countries; and as a result this 'Society' attracted all sort of people from different countries and with widely-varying characters. A host of fine yachts could be seen, many of whose owners knew little if anything about their yachts or about racing. Anthony Heckstall Smith, in his epic book *Sacred Cowes*, recounts the story of one owner who, when asked if he would like to take the helm from the skipper, replied 'No thank you, I never take anything between meals'.

'Gloster House', later to become 'The Gloster Hotel', facing the sea and with a commanding view of the racing, became the popular residence of the lords and ladies attending the sailing races. There they could sit and watch not only the racing but the elegant personalities passing below. In 1851 the schooner *America* sailed across the Atlantic, and in answer to a challenge succeeded in beating our finest yachts in a race around the Isle of Wight. Seven years later, in 1858, the 'castle' at the mouth of the river

Rainbow

13

was purchased and the Royal Yacht Squadron raised its flag for the first time on the flagstaff that is still there today, the mast of the original yacht *Bloodhound*. 'The Squadron', as it became known, was the most exclusive club of the day, and exclusively male, of course. Kings and princes of various nations were attracted to membership, amongst whom Emperor Louis Napoleon was a founder-member.

In 1888 my grandfather, Edward Beken, in residence as a chemist and druggist in Canterbury, Kent, decided to move his business to Cowes and establish himself in a house on the shore of the harbour at the mouth of the river; he told his elder son Frank that he too should work hard and graduate as a chemist—in those days one did as one's father said. The family business continued to prosper and, with the 'royal court' at Osborne House and the consequent demand for medicine, it was not long before the grand title of 'By Appointment to Her Majesty Queen Victoria—Chemists' was bestowed upon the business.

Frank Beken had by that time attained his pharmaceutical title and returned to Cowes to further his father's business. The premises had the unique advantage of having a large window overlooking the harbour and the whole Solent area, which was alive with the most shapely and elegant yachts from the boards of such classic designers as Nathaniel Herreshoff of America, Fife of Scotland and Nicholson of England, the whole scene being dominated by the Royal Yacht *Victoria and Albert*. It was at this time that an idea passed through his mind: 'Why not photograph this scene afloat, photograph each yacht in action and record them for ever?'

The thought was easier then the deed. How was it to be done? The only craft one could photograph from in those days were a steam pinnace, or a sailing cutter, or a longboat. It was impracticable to shovel coal in a steam pinnace and photograph at the same time; to use a sailing cutter was unreliable— which left only a longboat or dinghy. So he bought a dinghy, and I think this was the first time that seawater started to flow through the veins of the family.

Imagine Cowes Week—that mecca of yachtsmen: the Royal Yacht moored in the Solent surrounded by three hundred yachts of up to 400 tons, anchored and about to raise sail; longboats rowed by crews dressed in white, plying continuously between the yachts and landing-quays; thousands of craftsmen employed in building and repairing; victualling craft sailing in and out of the harbour loaded with wines and food. Cowes Roads, that splendid area of water, starts to come alive, hundreds of yachts tacking and cross-tacking, blue skies and rolling cumulus clouds. . . . How one could have wished to be a Monet, capable of capturing this scene in oils as well as photographing it.

Imagine the big schooners, with a cloud of sail; ketches, yawls and cutters, all with their spinnakers lifting and curling as they sail past the mouth of the river. . . . The lines of their bows and delicate counter-sterns have more voluptuous curves than any woman and surely must compete with the ladies of any royal court. Who could fail to fall in love with this scene and record it for posterity? This is what Frank Beken set out to do.

Now we are in the year 1893. The Prince of Wales (later to become King Edward VII) commissioned the famous Scottish designer G.L. Watson to design for him a large racing-yacht to be called *Britannia*. When she was first seen by the 'experts' she was condemned as a 'hideous racing machine'—their eyes were used to the clipper bows of the yachts of the day and could not accept the 'spoon' bow of *Britannia*. She proceeded to win her first race by a large margin; 122 feet in length, with a waterline length of 87 feet, a mast of 175 feet, carrying 11,000 square feet of canvas, she raced against her contemporaries—*Satanita, Valkyrie, Calluna,* and the German Emperor's yacht *Meteor* (formerly *Volunteer*).

In 1901, on the death of Queen Victoria, King Edward VII went on racing as a relief from his affairs of state; and yachting from Cowes continued to flourish, establishing the little port with its attendant society to the court.

The German Emperor was an enthusiastic sailing yachtsman who, it is said, 'arrogantly commanded members of his court to race on *Meteor* whether they cared for the sport or not'. He had four *Meteors* in all, and it was *MeteorIV* that challenged King Edward's *Britannia* to a private race at Kiel, with both crews standing on *Meteor* to await the presentation of the cup. The German Emperor presented the cup, congratulating King Edward on his win. Taking a careful look at the cup, King Edward placed it on the stern of *Meteor* and kicked it into the sea, commenting ''Twas only gold plate'. That story was told to Frank Beken by the captain of *Britannia* and gives some idea of the enthusiasm and intense rivalry that existed between owners at that time. Owners gave handsome prizes and rewards to their crews when they won a race, and at the end of a season's successful racing as well, so the crews were affected by the same spirit.

Just nine years later, on the death of King Edward, *Britannia* passed into the hands of his son King George V, who was another great lover of the sea. He had devoted himself to the Royal Navy, and it was only natural that he became an enthusiastic yachtsman. He could often be seen at the helm of *Britannia*, racing against his competitors—*Westward* from America, Herr Krupp's lovely *Germania* and the King of Spain's *Hispania*.

It seems incredible that four years later, in 1914, despite all the German interest in racing and the Kaiser's visit to Cowes, the Royal Yacht should have been in the Solent, the King having just reviewed the Fleet, when England and Germany found themselves at war. Perhaps the kicking of the cup into the sea had angered the Kaiser more than was realised!

However, to return to 1909: all the crowned heads of Europe were visiting Cowes at this time—the kings of Sweden, Spain, Norway, the German Emperor—and, together with our own Royal Family, the scene was sparkling. It was in this year that the Tsar of Russia attended Cowes Week with his family in the *Royal Standart*, escorted by a cruiser and a battleship. Here I can quote from my father's personal memoirs: 'The *Standart* was guarded by a number of fast launches that circled her continuously day and night. I slipped in between two of them and took a photo of the Royal Yacht and was then chased off. One afternoon, to my surprise, the three daughters of the Tsar paid a visit to my pharmacy, surrounded by detectives and police; curiously, they bought all the bottles of perfume that they could pack into their pockets. It was only a few years after that the world was shocked by the terrible tragedy of the assassination of the whole of the Russian Family.' In those days it was usual for European monarchs to be able to walk the tiny streets of Cowes freely among the people, to converse with them and enter the tradesmen's shops without fear of molestation—and today, with few exceptions, it is the same.

Let us go ashore for a moment. The year is now 1910 (but it could be any year). The Royal Yacht Squadron with its magnificent starting line, a row of 21 polished brass cannon at its feet, is busily sending and receiving messages to and from the racing yachts, by semaphore. Royalty are settling themselves on to the exquisite lawns, dressed in elegant blue blazers, white trousers and white-topped yachting caps. The royal barges (brass-funnelled steam pinnaces) are plying between the 'steps', picking up the guests for the day's racing. At about 7 am the crews of the big yachts are already gathering the food and fruits of the world from the little grocer's shop at the top of 'Watchouse Slipway'—five *gallons* of cream for a big three-masted schooner, *Fantome;* six pounds of caviar for the German Emperor's yacht *Meteor;* four cases of spirits for *Westward;* six cases of burgundy for the King of Spain's yacht *Hispania*.

A few sailors from the naval escorting ships are still around, 'bog-eyed' after a heavy night's drinking in the *Three Crowns*, having missed the last liberty boat at midnight. (I remember with awe, as a child, seeing sailors emerge from the seething mass in the *Three Crowns*, reel across to the slipway opposite, vomit ten pints of beer into the sea, and then reel back to consume another ten pints. This happened all night and every night.) Officers of the ships, resplendent in their uniforms, are busily collecting mail and the hundred-and-one other things from shore—signals, messages, daily papers, programmes, wives, etc, to take aboard. The small cutters from the sail-making firm of Ratsey are ferrying repaired sails out to the big schooners, whilst from a pleasant residential area (called 'Discount Alley' by the local shopkeepers!) the Captains and Chief Stewards are making their way to the quays. The High Street is alive with enthus-

Susanne, 1908

iastic townspeople hurrying down to the 'Parade' for a grandstand view of the start of the day's racing. At 9 am the pubs have already opened; last-minute racing-clothing is still being purchased—oilskins, sea boots, sou'westers—for it looks as if it is going to be rough weather for today's race.

In Frank Beken's chemist shop, lined up ready for collection, are a row of medicine-chests all made of solid oak, finely varnished, with such famous names as *H.M.Y. Britannia, Sonia, Margharita, Waterwitch, Nyria* and *Hispania* printed in gold-leaf on the top. These chests were constantly being refilled, for in those days many limbs were damaged, fingers split and bones broken. All main sheets and indeed all ropes were sweated-in by hand—the day of the winch had not yet arrived. To hoist the mainsail, ten men climbed up the jib halyards, transferred themselves to the main halyard, and by their total weight the mainsail was slowly raised. Many

Frank Beken at work

accidents were caused by ropes whipping round arms and legs, so a large number of splints was always added to these medicine-chests. *Britannia's* medicine-chest is still kept in Beken's shop to this day.

At 10 am each morning Frank Beken, with a seaman friend, rowed his 14-foot dinghy out into the middle of the Solent to photograph these great yachts. Often only two chances presented themselves, one as the yachts were passing at the start of the race, and the other when they returned. The dinghy had to stem the tides whilst waiting for the yachts to return, and probably only twelve photographs were taken each day—but from this number were obtained the classic shots of *Rainbow*, *Waterwitch*, *Susanne*, etc. Examine the photo of *Rainbow* for a moment. Imagine a dinghy 14-feet long in that sea and the great schooner approaching, as Frank Beken said 'with the roar of an express-train', with a white bone in her teeth and the howl of the wind through the rigging. Younger readers will not know that there was a man, called a 'mast headman', standing at the intersection of the main crosstree on the foremast: imagine the danger of his position as the schooners came about, with flaying sheets and canvas. The mast headman was there to free any snagged ropes, and he and his colleagues were a special breed of tough seamen.

In 1911, the programme for 'His Majesty's Cup' reads:

Schooner *Meteor*	— His Imperial Majesty the German Emperor	400 Tons
Schooner *Cetonia*	— Lord Iveagh	295 Tons
Schooner *Germania*	— Herr Von Krupp von Bohlen	368 Tons
Schooner *Cicely*	— G. Cecil Whitaker	263 Tons
Schooner *Adela*	— Claude T. Cayley, Esq.	224 Tons
Schooner *Clara*	— Herr Max von Guilleaume	185 Tons
Schooner *Susanne*	— O. Huldschinsky, Esq.	154 Tons
Schooner *Hamburg*	— Hamburgischer Verein Seefahart	331 Tons

These were schooners only: there were also cutters and yawls all over 100 tons—what yachts to photograph! with their mass of sail and long, beautifully-designed hulls.

The camera that Frank Beken used to photograph this scene was a folding camera, with a wire-frame view-finder, a Ross Xpress lens of aperture of only F.8 and a speed of 1/150th of a second. The glass negatives were 6″ × 4″ slides, and the camera contained a sliding bellows. The whole thing was not suited for the sea at all, being light and delicate. There was, however, no alternative, for all cameras were designed for land and studio use. Frank Beken had had ideas about designing and making a camera specially for use at sea, when suddenly, in 1914, war was declared and all thoughts of going to sea to photograph had to be abandoned. However, he conceived the idea of suggesting to 'their Lordships at the Admiralty' that it would be valuable to them to have photographs of all existing naval warships (and those yet to be built) as a permanent record. The idea was accepted, and for four years, when required, Frank Beken photographed the ships, at sea from a dockyard tug (driven by paddles), developing his enthusiasm for his original idea of photographing yachts in future years as well as running his chemist business.

The conditions under which he worked were difficult by today's standards. Imagine a paddle-steaming tug of 1914 vintage in the English Channel, a 30-knot warship approaching: distance had to be prejudged accurately as it would have been impossible to have manoeuvered in the tug. Half an hour's wait whilst the warship turned on a reciprocal course, four photos to be taken, and then back to Cowes to attend to his business ashore. All the negatives from this period were kept by the Admiralty.

Finally the Armistice came, and with it once more thoughts of going to photograph on the sea for pleasure.

I was born in 1914, following a brother two years previously and followed by another two years later. My father now had three boys on his hands, a business to manage, and he had to find time to indulge in his original idea of photographing afloat. I remember he spent long and arduous hours at the small family business to raise his family.

One cannot help comparing those days with today. We children had to walk miles to school, while now fond parents take their children to school 'round the corner' by car to save time—time for what? However, at nine years old I went to boarding school in Sussex. I suppose it was a good school. We were made to work and play hard and spell properly (so different from today), and the food was basic with a surfeit of stewed prunes (necessary for one's bowels, we were told)—hence my intense dislike of them today. Holidays were, of course, wonderful, although I remember going out with an old fisherman and getting my first fish hook through the palm of my hand. I was taken to the doctor, who snipped off the eye of the hook and then calmly pushed the hook, complete with barb, out the other side of the hand—it was of course the only way to do it other than cutting the palm open, but it looked a bit frightening at ten years old.

Of my childhood days I remember many things: the kitchen table which lifted up and revealed the bath underneath, to be filled from two gigantic copper kettles heated on the kitchen stove close by; I remember my bedroom at the top of the house, with three long flights of dark stairs to reach the light-switch at the top and dispel the thoughts of ghosts, etc, on the way up; and I remember having to break the ice in the Victorian water-jug in the basin in the room before I could wash on a winter's morning.

Frank Beken with Mark I camera

Crew of *Soprano*, 1895

I remember the scream of my favourite aunt who, when swimming in the sea off East Cowes, bumped her head on a dead cat which was floating on the surface; I remember the farm, five miles into the country, where we spent many happy days watching the wheat being scythed by hand from the edge of the field inwards until there was only a small square left in the middle and then waiting to see the mad rush of wild rabbits which had been driven into the centre by the noise of the farmhands sharpening their scythes with their whetstones.

I also remember with trepidation watching the farmer bringing the bull to the farm-gate, to be tied up there while it had a bronze ring put through its nose—

'A ton of power surging by
With seven devils in his eye.'

I sat on the gate with one leg each side, prepared to beat a hasty retreat. I also recall with wonder seeing the farmer suddenly whip his hand down a hole in the ground and pull out a rabbit, alive and kicking, by the back legs, and with one quick flip of the wrist break the animal's neck.

In our garden, where most people had a toilet, we had a darkroom, converted from an old garden shed made of pitch pine, and I remember my father, it seems for ever, emerging from behind a dark curtain with dishes of large and fine photographs ready to be washed in large teak tanks of running water. But it was at school that I first appreciated the marvels of photography: in the cricket-ground there was a wooden hut—generously called a toilet—bare boards with a hole in the centre, and inside as dark as night. One day, seated and trying a forbidden cigarette, I suddenly noticed on the inside of the opposite wall the image of a man, upside down, approaching the hut: it was one of the teachers. This image was projected through a pinhole in the wooden side of the opposite wall of the hut: it was the perfect pinhole-camera—and in colour!

After seven years I left school after passing all the required examinations, and immediately started to serve as an apprentice in my father's shop, making up pills and suppositories by hand for their respective destinations.

Above the chemist business there were two complete floors of living accommodation, on the top floor of which, about 25 metres above sea-level, there was a small room overlooking the sea to the east. This was made into an enlarging room for making paper prints from negatives. A large bellows in a frame $10'' \times 8''$ was fitted horizontally to the window of the room, and the glass negatives were fitted into this frame by way of a sliding carrier close to the window; a $10''$ lens was fitted to the panel at the other end of the bellows, and a vertical screen on a horizontal track was used to project the image to the required dimension, using daylight as the light-source.

Daylight is of course the best light for photography compared with electric light, therefore why not use it where practical for enlarging? In this room the light on a bright day was intense and even, as the sea and sky reflected the sunlight to the window; the results were perfect; an enlargement of one metre square could be perfectly exposed in fifteen seconds with shading and general technique (this will still be found to be difficult today, even with all the modern apparatus available); using daylight instead of electric light gave an exceptionally high-quality result—at no expense!

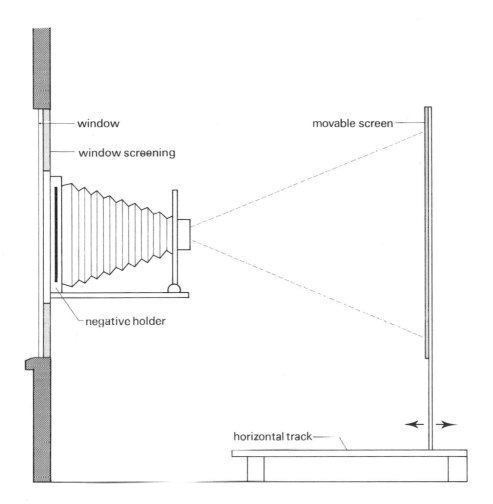

window

window screening

movable screen

negative holder

horizontal track

The Brooke, Isle of Wight, lifeboat, being hauled back to base

Building the
Mark I Camera

There is nothing more frustrating than having a good idea and not being able to put it into practice. My father was determined to produce fine photographs, but because of the poor equipment available it could not be done—it was like trying to make a piece of Chippendale or Louis Quinze furniture, with an axe. The bad points about the camera were:

1. It was too light to handle at sea.
2. The viewfinder was like a gunsight and each movement was transmitted to the camera.
3. One had to extend a bellows for focusing.
4. It had a focal plane shutter which started at speed nought and ended at 1/150th of a second so that half the negatives could be unsharp and the other half doubtful.

The only ways to improve this were

1. to eliminate the movement of the dinghy,
2. to find or make a faster shutter,
3. to use a larger camera with a larger negative and therefore reduce the degree of enlargement of the photographs.

There were no faster shutters available so that was impossible; the other two ideas were possibilities, and it was then that my father had his 'breakthrough idea'—he conceived the idea of firing the shutter with a rubber ball and tube, the ball being held between the teeth, not in the hand, while his two hands held the camera lightly, enabling the camera and himself to become one total gimbal. The camera should be virtually a wooden box, built of mahogany, and large enough to take a standard double 'bookform' slide size 8″ × 6″ at one end, with the shutter lens unit at

Keith Beken with
Mark II camera

27

the other. A simple box-type viewfinder with a lens at one end and a ground glass screen in the centre should be fixed to the top. At the end of the rubber ball and tube a release should be made, consisting of a tiny cylinder and piston, the piston to act as a hydraulic pump, actuated by biting the rubber bulb and so positioned that the lightest pressure of the bulb should fire the lever of the shutter. Two large brass handles, one on either side of the box, with the whole camera to be held practically at arm's length—it was here that the idea of the ball and tube held between the teeth came into effect. A movable front lens-unit, mounted on the front, focused by the simple turn of a wing nut, completed the whole concept. A 10″ lens, made by Ross of England, was the ideal lens, the 10″ focal length being correct for a 10″ × 8″ negative; and this lens could also be removed and used in the enlarger.

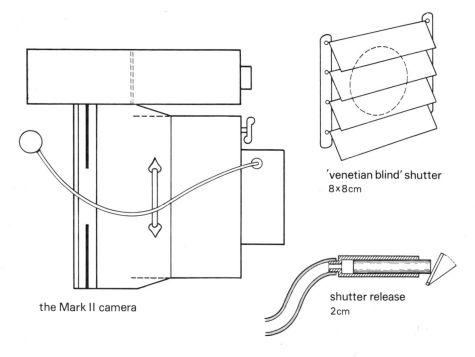

the Mark II camera

'venetian blind' shutter
8x8cm

shutter release
2cm

For the shutter unit, a 'Venetian blind' type shutter was conceived, to be mounted inside the camera just behind the lens, the shutter itself being tensioned by a clock spring on the outside and geared to the shutter on the inside. A model-maker employed by the shipbuilding firm of J.S. White at Cowes built the camera to the above specification. It was then painted, the brass handles added, the ball and tube fixed to the cylinder, the whole camera now weighing about six kilogrammes.

The method of focusing the camera was perhaps unusual: there were three distance-marks, which had been preset and marked thus: 'Dinghy' for close range, 'Cruiser' for medium range, 'Liner' for long range (infinity). When the image of a boat three-quarters filled the ground glass screen of the viewfinder, the shutter was fired.

Frank Beken then rowed out into the Solent and, standing up in the stern of the dinghy, 'shot' several pictures of the great racing yachts (one skipper remarked that the noise of the shutter being fired sounded like the starting gun). However, the idea of holding the camera at arm's length and firing the shutter by biting the rubber ball worked perfectly. Enthusiastically Frank rowed back to Cowes to develop his negatives—on each negative the horizon was absolutely level, which proved both that his idea of holding the camera at arm's length and the firing of the shutter was perfect, but the yacht itself was very slightly blurred, which meant that the shutter was still not fast enough. This was disappointing, since it was impossible to wind the clockspring any tighter; but the idea of the camera was a success and the firing of the shutter with the teeth was a real 'hair trigger'.

At the end of the racing season, when the camera was not in use, a new type of shutter was being advertised called the 'Adam's Shutter'. The diagram given below may not be quite accurate as I have reconstructed it them from memory, but the principle is correct. The shutter consisted of four leaves, kidney-shaped, each leaf being pivoted in the concave curve of

Royal Yacht Squadron, Cowes, 1900

the 'kidney'. It was a novel idea: when the shutter was released, the shape of the leaves and their centre pivot meant that each leaf only had to travel half the distance across the lens opening, one end of the leaf opening, and the other end closing, the aperture. This of course achieved a much shorter exposure of the negative and the shutter was therefore at least twice as fast

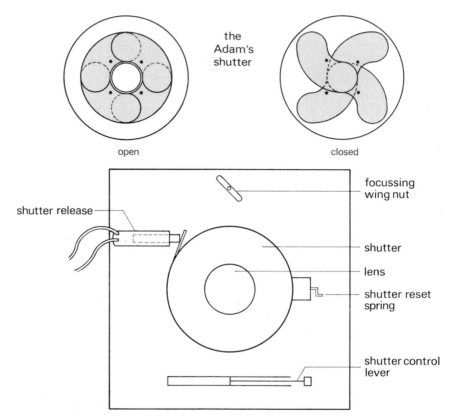

as any previous model with an estimated speed of 1/250th of a second. For a large shutter this was quite revolutionary, and it was fortunate that the Ross Lens, which was already in use, could with fine adjustment of the thread be fitted to this shutter.

The camera was accordingly taken to the workbench and the Venetian blind shutter stripped out, a new front panel screwed and glued into position, and the new shutter/lens screwed into place. The whole was then made light-tight and repainted. A new-rubber ball and tube were added to fit the tiny piston and cylinder as before, and the camera was once more taken to sea.

The camera seemed to be a success. Balancing on his toes, camera held in both hands, rubber ball in mouth, my father took many exposures as the big yachts raced by. The glass negatives were carefully developed, fixed and stood to dry: in the morning all negatives were sharp, all horizons level, all evenly exposed—all the hard work and imagination had produced good results.

My next three years were spent in London with occasional visits to Cowes; examinations came and passed; and finally the title of 'chemist and druggist' was awarded, enabling me to return to Cowes to attempt the art of keeping one eye on the dispensary and one on the sea. Becoming a chemist in a small country/seaside town in one's early twenties required many aptitudes—as a prescriber of medicine (most of the doctors were playing golf or sailing in the afternoons), a member of the local council, the shop becoming a cross between a confessional and a gossip-box—and one was called upon to do many things. In those days, the townspeople brought us their cats to dispose of when they had reached a great age. The method of disposal was basic, but, I think, kindly: the cat was put in a wicker basket, chloroform on a pad was added, and after a few minutes when the cat was in another world it was put in a sack, heavy weights were added, and it was then rowed out into the Solent and sent to join its friends at the bottom of the sea—almost a seaman's burial, in fact.

I remember one tough old tom-cat who, after being in the basket for thirty minutes with a strong dose of chloroform, when we opened the basket calmly jumped out, stretched its legs and walked away. It took half the bottle before that cat succumbed to the inevitable—I was learning many things as a chemist. . . .

Drugs and medicines seem basic by today's standards. I remember dispensing a large silver coated pill called a 'Number Nine'. It seemed to be used for everything from constipation to unrequited love. Veterinary products were also made by the local chemist, and I remember seeing in our prescription-book an entry reading 'HORSE BALLS'—a great pill about 3 cm in diameter, with basically the same constituents as the 'Number Nine', but about ten times stronger, with the direction: 'throw down the horse's throat—for colic, etc.'

With George V now King of England and racing *Britannia* with great enthusiasm at Cowes, the town kept its popularity; and it was not long before our chemist business received the distinction of 'Royal Appointment to His Majesty King George V—Chemists'.

Inevitably, any young fellow who lived by the sea had a natural inclination to sail on it; when the dinghy was not being used for photography, we three brothers rowed all over Cowes Harbour, exploring the Medina River and generally turning into water-rats. The dinghy had an iron centreboard, and it was not long before we fitted a mast with a gaff mainsail and a jib: the world was now our oyster, we foraged 'abroad' to England across the Solent, westwards to the Needles and eastwards to Spithead. Evening races were held by the Island Sailing Club and of course we had the urge to

compete: I asked Uffa Fox, who was then a young man living on a ferry-bridge in the river and well known for his enthusiasm for sailing, if he could find the time to give me a few lessons. He immediately jumped into the dinghy and gave me a first lesson. One evening a few weeks later, out in the Solent, he suddenly said, 'Well, Keith, you know all about it now.' With that, he dived over the side in shirt and shorts and swam ashore— half a mile away. This was my introduction to the inimitable Uffa.

On 9 July 1936, after the death of George V, I saw the Royal Yacht *Britannia* being towed past our garden by a destroyer to be scuttled out in the English Channel—a heartbreaking sight. The people of Cowes had seen this fine yacht since she was built in 1893. The sight of *Britannia*—still in fine condition but stripped of everything inside and outside—being towed out to be sunk was too much for some of the 'old salts' who had known her and raced her; but it was the will of King George V that, if none of his sons raced her, she should be scuttled—it was the end of a great era. Much of her running gear, mainsheet and jib-blocks, cleats, mast-hoops, tiller, racing- and prize-flags, etc, were bought by local people at an auction, and are still to be seen in various little houses in Cowes—I myself have a jibsheet block with *H.M.Y. Britannia* mounted on a small brass plate—a treasured possession, along with the medicine chest.

Meanwhile, we had got Ned Williams of Cowes to design us a launch which was to be built at his yard on the Medina. I spent many interesting hours watching every plank being added. She was carvel-built of pitch pine, 17 feet overall, an open launch with a small cuddy forward and a nice 'tumble home' to her stern. Given a Thorneycroft engine, she just managed eight knots; she was painted a particular shade of green that gradually became recognised by most yachtsmen afloat—this was to our advantage and theirs, as they knew that they did not have to worry about this small launch being in their direct path when they were racing. She became a fine sea-going launch in the roughest of weather, and the dinghy became her tender (serving us for sixty years before breaking up in a north-east gale).

Since about the age of 12 I had learnt how to handle ropes, how to make back-hand loop-splices, how to throw a heaving-line to its maximum length and, more important, how to catch one without receiving the heavy 'Turk's head' in the eye. When, as a child, you have a dinghy at the foot of your garden, on the sea, you absorb much knowledge.

◀
Rubin

Using the launch for photography, we found that we were going out in much rougher weather than previously, and this was having an effect on the quality of the photographs: they were becoming blurred again. This meant that we had once more to find some way of increasing the speed of the shutter. Stripping the shutter one winter's evening, we found that all four of its leaves were driven by a circular driving-chain. If a new big clockspring could be added, driving a cog-wheel to the chain, similar to our Venetian blind shutter, we thought it might be possible to attain an 'incredible' speed of 1/500th of a second.

After much work, with the help of a cycle engineer living next door, we put the whole thing together. It worked perfectly, all negatives were critically sharp, but the tension of the spring was enormous. Inevitably, nothing lasts forever (except perhaps all those empty plastic washing-up liquid containers littering our shores) and about three months later, whilst photographing, I heard a loud crack: the leaves of the shutter, which were made of Xylonite, had split in pieces. 'Back to the drawing-board': new leaves of thin stainless steel were made and once more the camera went to sea—perfect. The camera earned its living from then onwards, with the occasional replacement of a clockspring.

As we became used to it, the camera was so reliable that we needed to take only one photograph of each subject, safe in the knowledge that, barring accidents, it was exactly what we wanted. This was invaluable, for in order to take sixty photographs in a day we required thirty slides (two negatives each) and they were heavy and cumbersome. In those days we employed local boatmen to take the helm; and sometimes, through their particular taste for alcohol and resultant erratic helmsmanship, we made some hair-raising escapes from the path of high-speed naval craft and the fleet of liners which cruised in and out of Southampton Water.

The variety of subjects to be photographed made every one a challenge—flying-boats taking off, Schneider Cup seaplanes landing on the sea, torpedo boats approaching us at forty knots, and of course all the private yachts of various sizes and all under different conditions—this was the variety that made our job interesting.

The Schneider Cup Air Trophy race was at this time being raced by flying-boats from eight different nations. The difficulty in photographing them was that one did not know exactly when they would 'take off' from the sea—even the pilots did not know, for the sea conditions varied so much at the moment of lift-off. In later years seaplanes were raced five times round a circuit over the Solent, the most advanced designs being Italian. These seaplanes, being of small wing-area, had necessarily to 'land' on the sea at fast speeds and only in calm conditions: there were many hair-raising landings as the sea very often changed during the race from flat calm to choppy.

Torpedo-boats and gunboats or any fast naval craft were always the most exciting and challenging to photograph. The best and most impressive angle from which to take them is about five degrees off the bow: this means that one is virtually in the direct path of the oncoming craft, which is approaching at perhaps 40 or 50 knots. The technique is this: you take up position about a quarter of a mile directly ahead, cruising slowly on a straight course away from the gunboat, and at the same time signal him to accelerate. Fifty tons of wood and steel build up speed and head towards you; the scream of the turbines gets louder and the huge bow-wave spreading thirty feet each side gets closer, defying you to keep calm; your sphincter muscles tighten, but you keep on course. At a distance of fifty feet, with one eye in the camera and the other on the approaching boat, you gently edge off course away from him, shoot the picture, and immediately turn your stern to him as he passes. The huge wave lifts your boat, but you ride it as a cork on the sea. Everything is 'up and down', but softly; if you had turned into the wave (as most people do), it would slam your bow up, making camera and gin-bottles capsize. The gunboat then turns and repeats the procedure. As you once again slide away from him, the crew sometimes tend to follow your course instead of their own, watching you instead of their compass. This is really frightening, for to have fifty tons of steel at forty knots climbing over your transom is a sure passport to the next world.

Charles Nicholson, architect and boat designer, at the helm of *Candida*. *Cambria* and *Britannia* are in the distance

You have to have great faith in the reliability of your own boat, for under these circumstances an error of five degrees on the part of either helmsman could be catastrophic. At a distance of fifty feet, our launch disappears out of sight of the gunboat's helmsman—we are under his bow—and I have seen many an anxious look astern from him when he has passed us. Often they throw up a huge wall of water as they pass; and we quickly turn, receiving the thrash of water on our back—another good reason for having a wooden camera!

Whilst on the subject of positioning yourself when photographing yachts, etc, at sea, there are certain rules that must be observed:–

1) Never station yourself on the weather bow of an approaching small or medium sailing-yacht, for you disturb her wind and, if she luffs quickly, the possible resulting damage will earn you rude remarks—and justified ones, too.

2) Keep to the leeward and let the yacht approach you, for it is easier for

Edward VII boarding *Britannia*. The crew are in the rigging

you to bear away quickly, and safer, than to close on an approaching yacht when a freak wave may throw you into a collision course.

3) Never give any racing-yacht your wash: glide into and away, so that you leave a clean flat wake—helmsmen and crews will appreciate this, especially dinghy sailors.

I have always used what I would call 'standard' lenses on my cameras—that is to say, neither wide-angle nor telephoto—as I desire a true and accurate portrayal of the subject. This does not mean that no photographer should use the others for 'special effects'. Miniature cameras of the 35 mm type I abhor—having lit the firework, now stand back!—for many reasons. Firstly, they are too light to handle in rough weather. Secondly, they give too small a negative for a critically sharp enlargement of, say, 3′ × 2′. Every flaw, fingerprint and dust-spot is enlarged many times, and the cost of retouching flaws on photographs is time-and-money consuming. Finally, and perhaps worst of all, sea-water plays hell with them; and the number of expensive cameras lying around ruined because of salt-spray must run into hundreds. Do not believe what 'they' say—dropping them in fresh water or oil immediately is no good. 'But', you may ask, 'that great big black box you use, surely?'—well, let me explain: working from a large negative, any flaw, scratch, or dust spot, can easily be retouched, and a large original negative will give large, sharp enlargements. Heavy? Yes, for it is much more stable at sea and easier to gimbal than a light object held in both hands. For example, if you had to drive across a rough sea with a glass of water held in your hands, you would have very little left after a few minutes; do the same with a bucket of water, and you would have at least three-quarters of it left. An additional factor is that the camera is made of wood so that, apart from the action of sea water on it (which is little), you can rub it down with wet/dry sandpaper and repaint for next use. It is also big enough to hide inside if you really become frustrated with the rest of the world.

Interior of *Galatea*

The Big Class

Cowes Week, 1934/35—the days of the Big Class, with such yachts as *Whiteheather, Shamrock, Britannia, Endeavour, Velsheda,* etc; the ex-23 metres and the 'J' class with masts as tall as Nelson's Column—what names to conjure with, and what subjects to photograph! Come with me and observe! On any and every day the first race is at 10 o'clock. By 8 o'clock the crews have already been ashore and returned, as a minimum of two hours is needed to stow and hoist all canvas and prepare for racing. We in our darkroom are laboriously loading our slides in total darkness, thirty slides in all, sixty glass negatives altogether, all to be dust-free with no fingerprints on the glass negative. The slide-boxes are now full, the cameras ready, rough weather clothing donned, and we row out to the launch.

We hope the engine will be kind and start at once, for we have no self-starter and the magneto objects to moist air. We flood the carburettor and wind the starting-handle, followed by oaths, followed by the unscrewing of the plugs, wiping and drying, replacing, more winding—it starts! Gallons of petrol are lifted aboard (12½ pence per gallon then), we cast off mooring and gently ease the launch through the mass of yachts tacking out of the harbour to the line. The 'perfume' of bacon and eggs greets us as we filter through the late starters (why is it that food and drink smell and taste so much better on the water?); the light north-westerly air promises a strong breeze later; the day will be bright, cumulus clouds abound in a blue sky; the forecast is good.

The boom of the preparatory gun at 9.30 hrs from the Royal Yacht Squadron Line signifies the half-hour to the start. The course is indicated

Endeavour II, 1935

41

by a string of flags, and the course number shows us a westerly course, first mark at Lymington Spit buoy. The schooner *Westward* and the 'J' class are restlessly easing themselves into position; the tide is flowing east at two to three knots. At 9.50 another boom from the cannon, and already we can see them coming for the start on a long straight line for the outer mark-buoy. At 9.55 the five-minute cannon booms and throws cordite upon us as we wait just below it. We want to be just under the lee bow of the boats as they hit the line. Two minutes to go, and six 'J' class, each about 120' long, slice their way down the line, all starboard tack, a few feet between stem and stern. Boom crashes the cannon. *Endeavour,* within almost a stone's-throw of the rocks off the 'Squadron', screams for 'Water!' and proceeds to come about. The noise is deafening, the three jibs thrash, the main 'cracks' across and the blocks rattle. Away they all go on the port tack, hugging the shore to escape the flood-tide.

With us, all is action. We thread our way through these unleashed greyhounds, taking photographs as fast as possible, for it is only minutes before they are out of reach of our lenses, as they are probably travelling at fifteen knots to our maximum of eight. Suddenly they come about again, twenty men haul their mainsheets in, another ten are handling the stay-sails and jibs, sweating to get the last inch of the sheets in. Suddenly *Velsheda,* all 120 feet and 200 tons of her, touches bottom—cries of 'Water' and once more the rattle of thunder as they all come about again and head down westwards. Meanwhile we are drenched in spray and green seas, bruised and battered, for the wind has risen and the waves thrown up by these big class are not kindly.

They draw away from us and for 10 minutes we rest, wipe the salt out of our eyes, our lenses, our cameras, just as excited as the skippers and crews of these great yachts, for the action has been stirring, difficult, and at times 'hairy'; but we know that in that black box of ours are some classic pictures. Ten minutes later another start; next class ten minutes later; another and another and another. *Westward*—the long, lean, elegant schooner designed by American Francis Hereshoff—had been a late starter, having had some difficulty in reefing her main; but now she came smoking past in unleashed fury, tramping iron-hooved over the short seas that were building up in the vicious squall which suddenly blew. With the crew still beating in the reefs and twenty men on the mainsheet, it could well be her day to beat the rest of her class—the 'J's'. On a rough day such as this, *Westward* always looked for extra crew for the sheets and she had picked five young enthusiasts from 'Watchouse Slipway' (vulgarly called the 'Spit and Lean' by the locals). One old retired skipper muttered to me as they were going aboard, 'There go the lambs to the slaughter'. I did not get the message—until six hours later, when they were rowed ashore, and the hands of the five extra crew were raw and bleeding. They had been put

Westward

on the mainsheet during the race by the skipper, T.B. Davis, who was known as a tough character; and one day's racing after 51 weeks of wielding a pen in an office had taken its toll. On *Westward's* mainsheet there were six blocks, three or four-sheaved each, which meant 'sweating-in' many yards of sheet to gain a foot; and probably the old hands had eased their own labour a little and made the new boys work their guts out. There were no winch 'coffee grinders' in those days.

Victoria and Albert: the royal yacht launched by George V

About three hours later, the big class can be seen in the distance returning from the west, all approaching at thirteen knots under a cloud of sail, spinnakers flying and main booms lifting and straining at the mass of rope and blocks and sheets. We, with our maximum speed of only eight knots, have to intercept them, for we have only one chance of a photo, just one correct angle at which to take them —and this interception is not easy. How many times have I cursed our engine for not being just a little bit faster! Come in really close with me as one of these 'J's' passes: the deck is cleared, a few men up for'ard tending the sheets, the rest, all down aft, grouped round the wheel. Sandwiches (smoked salmon and cucumber?) and gin and tonic are being consumed, owner and friends in blue jackets and white caps and trousers, the crew in white duck racing-clothes. We lower our heads as we pass under the mainboom, friendly waves from the crew and one points skywards—we look upwards to see a small tear in the top of the spinnaker. As we watch, there is a 'Whiissh' and the spinnaker splits from top to bottom. With no fuss, the helmsman shouts a word, the foredeck crew leap up, and the afterguard carry on with their gin and tonics, there being another half an hour before the next mark.

Eventually we have to return to the shore. I hate leaving the scene: when you race yourself, you become so enthusiastic with the tactics, etc, that you forget that you are not out for pleasure alone—there is work to do. By five

45

o'clock we are in the darkroom, plates developed, four at a time in separate dishes; by the time they are fixed, washed and put to dry, the slides reloaded and everything prepared for the next day, it is midnight. Proofs have to be made for the next day for the crews to inspect and make disparaging comments about the other competitors. Inevitably, of course, our camera sometimes breaks down, and the midnight oil is burnt to repair it before the next day. In those days you became photographer, engineer, seaman and camera-repairer; it was necessary to be all these to become a marine photographer.

After Cowes week ended the 'J' class sailed down to Torquay for a week's racing and then later to the Clyde. In 1933 I had the good fortune to see an epic race off Babbacombe and Torquay in Devon. The participants were *Velsheda* (the 'Woolworths' boat' to the locals, as she was owned by the managing director of that firm), *Shamrock* (owned by Lipton), *Astra*, and *Britannia,* skippered and helmed by Philip Hunloke, the King's sailing master. The wind was freshening with a gale promised, *Velsheda* and *Shamrock* had reefed, and *Britannia* and *Astra* were carrying full mainsail. On the second round of the triangular course the gale struck. *Velsheda* and *Astra* retired in difficulties, and *Britannia* approached on a terrific reach, with her main and staysails eased well off. She must have been at her maximum of fifteen knots; her entire lee-deck was awash to the deckhouse (and, her beam being 23′, it meant that ten feet of her deck was under water), the water hitting her lee rigging and cascading over the deckhouse. The crew were all snugged down on the weather rail and Philip Hunloke at the wheel obviously had all he could do to hold *Britannia* on her course. *Shamrock* then lost her mast—a good hundred feet of it over the side— leaving *Britannia* to roar her way through the squalls to the finishing line. It was *Britannia's* day and weather; and the old boat, built in 1893, showed her younger competitors what she could do. At all regattas, when the weather was rough, the local people were always heard to say 'This is Britty's day'. King George relished hard sailing, and together with Philip Hunloke as master he could be seen at the wheel, taking time off from matters of state.

Astra crosses the finishing line at Harwich

This, then, was my life up to 1939—dispensing, and the hundred-and-one things involved in conducting a pharmacy, and being a marine photographer as well: *quelle combinaison!* Now, whenever there is a 'high' over England there is usually a 'low' coming in from Iceland or the west or somewhere. This time it came from the east-south-east—Germany. War was declared in September. Immediately all boats of every description were prohibited from going afloat, and worse was to follow. Many boats were requisitioned by the Navy, my 14′ sailing dinghy being one of them. The launch oddly disappeared—I cannot remember how—but it was miraculously 'found' in a haystack somewhere by my father in 1945.

World War II

1939. Again, glancing through my father's memoirs, his thoughts are revealed. 'Looking back over fifty years, it seems that the world has been continuously at war, my father remembered the Franco-Prussian War of 1870, followed by the war between Spain and America, followed by Russia and Japan, the Boer War, Italy and Ethiopia, World War I, and now World War II'. All this to be followed, of course, by India and Pakistan, America and Vietnam, the Middle East, Angola and the troubles of Rhodesia.

Yachts were stored in sheds, and motor yachts commandeered and used as patrol vessels for coastal convoy. Liners were converted to armed merchantmen and virtually no civilian was allowed on the sea. The sailmaking firm of Messrs Ratsey and Lapthorn of Cowes and Gosport was converted to making barrage balloons, and the yacht and shipyards were busy making lifeboats and every possible type of boat to Admiralty contracts. Messrs J.S. White & Co on the Medina River at Cowes went on full-time building destroyers for the Navy and repairing other ships of the allied navies.

What is it that makes one wish to volunteer to join one of the armed services in wartime? Many things, I think: a wish to help one's country, an escape from normal life, a glance into the unknown? Who knows? War cuts into one's life. One has no idea what is going to happen in the future and for how long. What happens in a war? Only people who have known it really know. My father, who had been kept on the 'Home Front' as a chemist to minister to the sick, could only say what happened in the last war when bombs were dropped by hand by enthusiastic pilots, and later

The Shetland coast in winter

HMS *Intrepid*, 1937

▶

Cynara

from Zeppelins. I remembered the explosion and conflagration of the airship R101 from my earlier days, and somewhere between 1936 and 1939 I remember the German *Graf Zeppelin* which flew low along our South coast from Cornwall to Kent, no doubt busily taking photographs (on a peaceful flight) over our coastline and the Naval Dockyards of Plymouth and Portsmouth. When it passed over Cowes I was walking in the High Street and it flew so low that I remember looking up and finding the sky completely blotted out.

However, within one week of volunteering for the Navy I was called to the colours in the Royal Air Force—a good start—and I became the lowest form of animal life (Aircraftsman 2nd Class), being issued with a uniform too big and boots too small. One very soon learns how to exist in the forces. For instance, we were all due for an injection of anti-typhoid serum the next morning—after the injection you immediately faint thereby having the rest of the day off free. There being no hot water in the sleeping quarters, you used your second mug of hot tea at breakfast for shaving (without sugar and milk)—it also gives you a good tan! You learn very quickly. . . .

I shall not write of the horrible things that one sees and does in a

war—there are plenty of books on that. Instead I'll write of the amusing things that happened—and without a sense of humour I would have been completely lost. After two months of scrubbing out thirty lavatories twice daily, I was 'posted' to a hospital in the Fen District on the East Coast. As there was a minimum of sleeping accommodation in the hospital, we were billetted with various local people. I had the good fortune to be with two generous people. I discovered that in his spare time the husband was a poacher, and we had many profitable evenings in the 'dykes' (ditches running through the fields about five feet deep) where we shot partridge with .22 rifles fitted with silencers. Retribution followed one very dark night when crossing a road in nil visibility. Groping my way across and just making out the white line which I thought was the centre of the road, I took half a dozen firm steps to reach the pavement and dissappeared into a dyke on my head, the 'white line' being the edge of the pavement. This put me in hospital for a week. From my bed I was able to witness an 'amusing' event in the life of one of the new male nursing orderlies, a young fellow who had been told by the Matron of the hospital always to warm a bed-pan before placing it under the patient. This night he did so—by putting it in the oven first, and then under the patient. . . . I leave you to imagine the result.

The hospital was in a little village, by name Littleport, five miles from Ely in the heart of the Fenland where the countryside is so flat that you could see a steam train approaching five miles away, and could time yourself to the second for that last beer before your five-minute converging course to the railway station. On Christmas Eve, I and a 'buddy' hitch-hiked to London, lying in the back of a Ford 3-ton truck amongst six sides of raw beef. We emerged in London after four hours looking like, and smelling like a butcher's shop, to celebrate Christmas with our parents. The next evening we had to return to our base, arriving at Ely at Midnight in a carpet of snow. The five-mile walk in the night was long, but under a brilliant moon we saw the most wondrous scene of Ely Cathedral, the old town, trees, hedgerows and fields, all under a mantle of snow, a clear starry sky and perfect silence—a scene that is to me as fresh as yesterday.

In April 1940 I was sent to Torquay on the south coast, to the Palace Hotel which had been taken over by the RAF to be used as a hospital for officers. My job was to equip this hospital with all its medical and surgical requirements. The bar became the dispensary, the cocktail lounge the medical stores, the refrigerator held the blood and the badminton court became the morgue. It was the time of the 'phoney' war, the hospital packed with doctors and surgeons waiting for patients, and, in the absence of any, examining all the staff to see if there was anybody on whom they could practise their art. One of the office staff was found to have an undescended testicle—needless to say he was immediately placed on the

◀

Brave Swordsman

53

slab and the mystical operation performed.

After six months of this, and bored with inaction, I applied for my commission to become an officer in the hope of seeing some action and doing more for the war effort. My commission was granted, and after two months of vigorous training, on returning to Torquay, I was immediately posted from the sunny south to the cool North—the Shetland Isles, 100 miles north of Scotland. Well, at least I was surrounded by sea. On the southernmost tip of Shetland there was a small village called Sumburgh, the one and only large hotel had become the Officer's Mess, and an airstrip had been built to take fighter aircraft and medium/small bombers. My job (having had some previous training) was to brief pilots on their strikes across to Norway, which had then been overrun by the enemy.

1940. The Shetland Isles in winter are no sinecure, the weather is hard and tough, dawn is about 10 am and dusk about 4 pm, and it blows like hell in a gale (of which there are many, sometimes at 100 miles per hour, when even the seagulls have difficulty in flying). To give some idea of the force of the winds, two Sunderland flying-boats of Coastal Command were blown underwater at their moorings in the Orkney Isles, 75 miles further south.

My task in the Operations Room of flying control was to supply all pilots with meteorological reports, courses, rations, survival kits, call-signs of the day, details of enemy aircraft and silhouettes of enemy warships—the *Tirpitz, Prinz Eugen, Gneisenau* and *Scharnhorst*, which were suspected of being hidden in the Norwegian fjords after the sudden dash of the three latter from Brest through the English Channel. A squadron of Spitfires flown by Norwegian pilots, the aircraft stripped of everything except cameras, and with extra fuel tanks, flew each day to the tip of Norway and then streaked south down the coast at a low altitude over the fjords. These flights were extremely dangerous, due to enemy anti-aircraft gun-fire and fighters, but no guns were carried by these Spitfires, to save weight. Many times they landed back at base with virtually only a carburettor-full of petrol; often the cockpit hatchcovers were blown off by anti-aircraft guns and the pilots were frozen on their return. A squadron of Blenheim bombers was also stationed at Sumburgh. These covered approaching convoys from the west and were also used to attack the enemy air-bases at Stavanger in South Norway.

On days when there was no flying and the base could relax for a few hours, I took the opportunity of exploring the islet. The coast was infinitely rugged and when the gales blew from the West the spindrift was carried completely across the island. This, coupled with the fact that there was a lighthouse at the southern tip of the island, with a loud foghorn which blew every minute, gave one the impression of being on a huge ship at sea, especially when the visibility was nil. Seals abounded off the coast and

Meteor

were almost human in their actions, with their big eyes and realistic
moustaches. Three or four of them would accompany you, swimming
almost alongside, as you walked along the white sandy beaches.

I found the bird-life interesting. The whole island teemed with eider
duck (the feathers of which make your real eiderdowns). They nest
virtually on the rough ground and will not move off their nests when you

approach. Many times I almost inadvertently stepped on them, since their colouring blends perfectly with the peat on the ground.

The fulmar (even the name is delicate) is a gentle bird, all white, which seems to glide incessantly without moving its wings; when you are walking along the cliff edge, these birds quietly approach you from behind and gently touch you with their wingtips as they pass.

The *big* birds are the black-backed seagulls, huge gulls with a wingspan of two metres. They are extremely vicious when aroused, and will attack you in long sweeping dives and low fast approaches from behind rocks, striking at you with their beaks (it is useful to wear a hat). They also have a nasty habit, in the lambing season, of diving on the baby lambs, frightening them towards the water's edge, and then picking them up and carrying them off in their beaks. Many times I carried a .22 rifle to drive them off their foul work.

Sheep, of course, was the main 'industry'—for producing genuine Shetland wool. A Shetland collie dog used to attach itself to me on my walks—the farmer having left his dog all day by itself in charge of the sheep. At dusk the dog would automatically round up the sheep and return them to the fold; I found that if I lifted an arm the dog would rush away and bring all the sheep around my feet. One day I paid a visit to Lerwick, the capital of Shetland, a bustling fishing port and centre for the dispatching of the sheep of the islands. It was a typical North Sea fishing port, cold and hard living (how life must have changed today with oil-rigs in profusion lying off its shores). Walking through its narrow streets on this occasion, and being always curious in any new place, I wandered up a side street, and saw a very long low building, of such length that I could not imagine what was inside. Seeing two large open doors, I casually poked my nose round the door and received the shock of my life. Inside, in two long rows were about 200 sheep, lying on their backs with their legs in the air, throats cut and the blood draining into a long open trough stretching from one end of the building to the other—ugh!

However, if one is not curious, how does one learn? I had noticed, on the drive through the narrow roads to Lerwick, what appeared to be cut wood stacked around cottages—and yet it did not look like wood. Stopping off at a cottage I examined it more closely and found it to be cut cubes of closely fibrous material stacked in such a way as to be easily dried in the permanent winds that always seem to blow in Shetland. It was the first time I had seen peat. It is cut in squares out of the surface of the ground with sharp-edged spades, stacked to dry, and then burnt in ovens for cooking or heating water and also for huge open fireplaces in the cottages. It burns fiercely with intense heat, giving out a wonderful aroma that makes you dream of the little cottage in the country that we all want, away from the rat-race of today. Peat is of course the transition of the forest's wood to coal, and one wonders in Shetland how many thousands of years ago the trees and hedges disappeared, for there is no sign of either today.

1941. Early Spring came; reconnaissance flights continued to be flown in the clearing weather down the Norwegian coastline; the Operations Room staff, deep underground, were quietly plotting their aircraft on the board. Mugs of the inevitable tea with powdered milk were continually being supplied to the team with their eyes glued to the screen, showing the minute-by-minute progress of our aircraft. The air in the room (if there was any) was full of the disgusting smell of wartime cigarettes which contained anything but tobacco. A radio was quietly playing a disc of Vera Lynn (the sweetheart of the Forces)—suddenly an R/T message hit the air '*Tirpitz* in Trondheim. . . . *Tirpitz* in Trondheim. . . . *Tirpitz* in. . . .' silence.

Immediately everything was galvanic action, radio messages flew, telephones were scrambled, Air Ministry and all Combined Services were informed. Continual flights were then flown to Trondheim from first light to last light day after day after day. Spitfires and Mosquito aircraft, stripped of everything except a camera, flew fast and low below the enemy radar. The first pilot who had spotted her was brought in for questioning. 'Where was she exactly? Had she torpedo nets around her? What other craft were in the fjord?' and a thousand other questions. His film was processed and there was the *Tirpitz*, the pride of the German Navy, moored close under the steep side of the fjord on one side and protected by anti-torpedo and anti-submarine nets on the seaward side.

Now that the enemy knew that they had been spotted, our aircraft were met with an absolute barrage of anti-aircraft fire from the ship, and fighters from their ground stations. Our airfield was continually attacked, the enemy coming close in behind our landing aircraft, endeavouring to shoot them down at this most vulnerable moment. Our radar showed aircraft returning, but we had difficulty in differentiating between enemy and friendly. It was the Commanding Officer's dog, a big Irish setter, who knew when enemy aircraft were close, for he made a great leap under the plotting-table, his ears having picked up the sound of enemy engines, which he knew were immediately followed by bombs or cannon-fire. He really became our 'Early Warning Radar'.

Torpedo-carrying aircraft came up from Scotland, refuelled and waited for 'strike weather'; six 'Swordfish' aircraft (affectionately know as 'Stringbags') arrived, and were held for two days. The evenings were convivial, the tables in the Mess stacked one above the other, and each pilot climbed to the top in bare feet and imprinted his bare footprints in ink on the ceiling. Next day they set off to strike at the *Tirpitz* and were never seen again. It was understood that they had hit a snowstorm on the way, iced up, and the whole six aircraft lost—twelve of our finest young fliers.

A week later, six Beaufort torpedo-carrying craft landed from Scotland to refuel for a strike. Late one afternoon, to arrive at dusk, the six aircraft set off. They hit terrible weather across the North Sea: two reached their target; two were forced back to Scotland; one crashed in the Shetland hills having been forced back at night; and the last, with the Commanding Officer of the Canadian Squadron on board, managed to land back on our airstrip at midnight, skidded on the ice into wooden buildings at the edge of the runway, and ended up with the nose of the aircraft gently pushing open the door of a lavatory where one of the ground staff was sitting on the seat.

Then the aircraft caught fire, but the crew managed to escape. The pilot calmly put his hand on the torpedo, walked quietly back, and said, 'I think we had better get the hell out of here'. Everybody fled like rabbits, with not a wall, not a tree nor even a blade of grass to hide behind. In three minutes the torpedo blew up and just about everything was blown flat. But the boys had done their job—two aircraft reported that they had managed to put torpedoes deep into the hull of the *Tirpitz* and stopped her from sailing and attacking our convoys for many months.

I was due for a week's leave. Cadging a lift on an aircraft to Aberdeen, I managed to get another lift on an old Handley Page 'Harrow' transport aircraft to Doncaster. Two things I vividly remember on that trip. Looking out of the windows of the aircraft, I noticed large strips of fabric peeling off the starboard wing and disappearing astern. The pilot did not seem to worry, saying that it sometimes happened with these old fabric-covered aircraft. As we circled Doncaster before landing, I saw an interesting and thought-provoking sight—the whole city was completely ringed with huge bomb-craters, a sight that was never shown to the public during the war.

By the time I reached Cowes I had just three days' leave, as I had to allow at least two days to get back to the Shetland Isles again, with the improbability of jumping an aircraft all the way. Three days later, then, I made a long and tiring train journey, blacked out overnight to Aberdeen, where fortunately I had a spare seat in a Beaufighter aircraft being piloted as a replacement. We were to follow another Beaufighter to the Isles as we had no guns, no protection, and no compass. Halfway there, we flew into a snowstorm and, on emerging, found that we had lost our guide; this was not amusing as we had no compass and were completely unarmed. However, the pilot unconcernedly took us up another 3,000 feet, and in ten minutes we could see in the distance what appeared to be a tiny strip of something that was not sea but our islands. In fifteen minutes we were home and dry.

Titanic leaves Southampton, 15 April 1912

HMS *Jersey*, built by J. Samuel White in Cowes, 1935

▶
After the war: HMS *Vanguard*, with RORC racing yachts alongside

Air~Sea Rescue

It was here in Shetland that I began to be restless at just watching events and really feeling unable to satisfy my mind that I was doing enough. I felt the senselessness of the single German fighter that came over and shot dead the single occupant of the lighthouse on the tiny island of Fair Isle between Shetland and Orkney Islands, and I was moved by another instance of listening to the R/T in the Operations Room when a young sergeant pilot of a Blenheim bomber was returning to base from Norway. He had been badly shot up over Stavanger and was nursing his aircraft across the sea; within a few miles of Shetland we heard his voice on the R/T—'Position 15 miles, 110°, losing height'. A few minutes later came 'Losing more height', and a minute later 'Losing height fast, won't make it'; and then silence. I was allocated the duty of going through his personal effects and the notes that he had written before the 'strike' leaving his small belongings to his loved ones. . . .

All these happenings stirred me deeply; I wanted to do something more positive, and it was then that we received a signal asking for officers who had knowledge of the sea to apply for the Air-Sea Rescue (Marine). The lives of valuable pilots and crews were being lost by 'ditching' in the sea and there were not enough rescue craft to reach them quickly. Now this was something that I wanted to do something about, and I immediately applied for an interview at Air Ministry, London. Within days I had an interview before a galaxy of Air Commodores, and with gentle persuasion I told them what a fine fellow I was—a man of the sea, etc. They evidently believed me for within one week I received a signal to proceed on a week's leave and then report to 'Air-Sea Rescue—Stranraer' in Scotland for a course of instruction.

My last evening in Shetland was a riotous one—much drinking and toasting and chaffing of the 'Met Officer', who inevitably, like all the others of his breed, never seemed to produce an accurate weather forecast. In the Officers' Mess he was caught with that old trick where a funnel is placed in the waistband of the trousers, you bend your head back, place a coin on your forehead, and slowly, by inclining your head forward, you make the coin drop into the funnel. It looks very easy, and the Met Officer immediately wanted to do it. Placing the large funnel in the top of his trousers he bent his head back, placed the coin on his head, and immediately four glasses of beer were poured into the funnel by the onlookers—hilarious.

A Flight Lieutenant who had been in the Shetlands for two years and had been trying to get a posting elsewhere—anywhere—to the Middle East if necessary—to get away from the Shetland Isles (with no success) begged me to try and do something for him. I told him to start paying open and wild compliments to the Commanding Officer's wife. I heard later that he was posted within one week to the South of England—it never fails!

Arriving at Stranraer, I was immediately given a free pass for leave and returned to Cowes for a week.

Cowes had had some vicious bombing. At midnight the enemy would bomb and then return again two hours later when the fires were burning bright. The target had presumably been J.S. White, the builders of naval destroyers. The enemy had not succeeded in obliterating their target, and most of the bombs had dropped on the town. All the windows of my father's pharmacy had been blown out and all the bottles were lying in pieces on the floor. The whole area was cordoned off for a week as a precaution against delayed-action bombs. There was a great mess to clear up, and after helping in this I had to return to Stranraer.

Rubin, 1958

We slept in nissen huts in the woods, without heat, and underwent a full day's training at sea, learning Morse Code, signals, handling boats at sea, urgent First Aid treatment with special application to the sea, navigation by 'dead reckoning', coding and decoding, and all the requirements necessary to be in charge of eleven men on your own craft at sea in wartime. Six weeks of this was enough, and then we were posted to the various marine craft stations.

In the early evening whilst on the course I took the opportunity of walking through the countryside: it was full of pheasant and hare. One particular evening I remember well, I was walking down the edge of a small forest. Turning the corner, I suddenly saw two pheasant in the corner of the field, feeding; on each side of them was a high wire fence and very tall pine trees. They immediately saw me and rose quickly and vertically, like a helicopter, for thirty metres in the air and then over the

trees. I have never seen such a wonderful and inspiring example of flight. At dusk the hares literally behave like the proverbial 'Mad Hatter' of *Alice in Wonderland*—they bolt from their holes into the fields, stand on two legs, box each other, leap into the air and generally behave as though possessed with the devil. It was a rare and fine sight.

Leaving Stranraer, I was posted to Calshot Air-Sea Rescue Base at the mouth of Southampton Water—this was really a case of putting a round peg in a round hole. I was given the rank of Flying Officer and became 'No 2' on a 42-foot 'Scott Payne' high-speed launch to operate in the English Channel. These HSLs had a top speed of 40 knots and were powered by two Napier Sea-Lion engines. They were very lightly built and contained as little equipment as possible to enable them to make a fast, sure rescue. Our main 'enemy' at this time was the 'Walrus' single-engined sea-planes flown by the Royal Navy. They could reach survivors more quickly than we could, and we heaped abuse on them as they picked the prize out of the sea from under our noses—but at least the intense rivalry ensured that the survivor was safely and quickly rescued.

I was then given my first command, to go to Brightlingsea on the east coast, take my crew of eleven and commission a 20-metre long-range rescue boat, which was just about to be launched. She was hardchined, almost flat-bottomed, with about 5 metres' beam. Three Perkins diesel engines, a huge cabin (used as a sick bay) aft, and three fuel tanks gave us about three days' searching without refuelling. We nosed out to the east coast, navigating our way past the cemetry of shipping that had been sunk by the enemy, all British ships with their masts showing above the surface, a cruel reminder of the E-boat war that was being waged in this particular area. Our first port of call was Ramsgate, Kent. A full southerly gale was blowing, and trying to negotiate the narrow harbour entrance was like trying to thread a needle in a gale of wind. I watched a 'N' class ML of 35 metres, used for fast convoy work, make a rush for the entrance: she cannoned off the harbour wall to port and disappeared inside.

We stood off and went in at fifteen knots like an arrow—and then had to put her full speed astern and hard to port to miss the 'middle ground' inside. The next day we set out for Calshot from Ramsgate. The gale had abated and had been replaced by thick fog. Reaching Beachy Head without seeing a thing, we then received a radio-message to return to Dover because of intense fog ahead. We turned 180 degrees and laid our course, arriving two hours later with Dover Western entrance 'dead on the nose'. I must say I was pleased with myself, for in going from Ramsgate to Beachy Head and returning to Dover in fog and with cross-tides, we had by pure navigation been 'bang on target'. Our subsequent voyage from Dover to Calshot was uneventful, and on arrival we kitted up with the hundred-and-one things necessary to render the boat operational. On duty, we would normally put to sea and make a rendezvous about five miles off the Nab Tower in the English Channel, covering strikes by our fighter aircraft on the French enemy-occupied coast; duties were two days at sea, followed by one day at base to re-victual and gather new signals and codes for the next trip.

Several of our sea-rescue craft had recently been shot at off the east coast. This, of course, was against international law, and we were instructed to fit a pair of Lewis guns port and starboard. Using them was like trying to shoot an aircraft with a catapult, and just about as effective. Our deck was painted bright yellow—the recognised colour afloat for non-combatant and rescue-craft. I later painted mine a camouflage green/blue colour, as yellow seemed to attract the enemy. Later on, the Air Ministry directed that this was to be done on all rescue-boats. Some craft were issued with an Oerlikon gun mounted on the stern. This gave some protection, and we had strict orders not to use it unless attacked. These guns were only issued to the faster boats as there was no position on the deck of the long-range craft for this size of gun. Our craft were very fine sea-going boats, and it was usually the crew who capitulated first in rough weather. I remember Richard Preston riding out a gale for three days off south-west Scotland and his boat performed perfectly. With their three Perkins diesel engines, they were very manoeuvrable; and with their low freeboard aft, picking up survivors from dinghies in rough weather was relatively easy.

A typical day at sea started at about 06.00 hours, first to the Nab Tower to wait. Suddenly a message would be flashed to us in Morse Code. 'Proceed 195 degrees, 50 miles.' The engine had meanwhile been kept warmed up, the course was laid off on the chart, and we were off at fifteen knots to the required position. On arrival at the estimated position a square search was made, first half a mile north, then a half mile east, then a mile south, then a mile west, continually increasing the distance on each leg to cover a wide area, all eyes and ears turned for the tiny rubber dinghy in the vast sea.

Our first rescue was that of a pilot who had baled out of a Thunderbird fighter. He was an American of the 'Eagle' Squadron, a squadron who had volunteered to fly with the RAF before America had come into the War. When we picked him up, he said in real American nasal twang, 'Gee, buddy, I'm sure glad to meet you. I was up there and felt my seat getting hot, so turned her over and baled out.' His aircraft had caught fire, and since his petrol tank was situated under his seat he decided to bale out instead of being blown out. We carry a gallon of rum aboard, for emergencies, and as we considered this an emergency we broached the cask and drank to the American Air Force, the Royal Air Force, and every other Force.

Arriving back at Calshot, I found a message to say that the whole

Air-Sea Rescue unit was to be moved to Cowes, *en bloc*. This was quite extraordinary—to be based in wartime at my home port. The base was to be part of Marvin's Yard, a little way up the Medina River. Some of the big old steam yachts were still lying on the mud alongside the base. The big slipway was to be used for hauling our boats up for inspection and running repairs, repainting, etc. New crews arrived occasionally, and others were posted to different units. Cooks for the galley were invaluable, and we took extreme measures to try and keep a good cook. The bad ones were always exchanged if possible. All types of fellows were sent to the unit as crews. They came from all walks of life—accountants, bank clerks, etc. I was given one fellow who had never been on a boat before in his life. One day I gave him an order to tighten-in a mooring rope and found him sweating hard to no avail—he had not untied the rope from the cleat . . . However, they were all soon licked into shape and became an enthusiastic team of willing fellows. Many of the volunteers came from all parts of England, a proportion having probably never even seen the sea before, but they showed plenty of courage in learning about it with its changing moods and conditions, no two days ever being the same.

Our sea-going clothes were adequate, but only just. In winter, sea-boots, submarine stockings and RAF battledress, an oilskin and—oh yes, a sweater. I always told pilots that we were certain to pick them up if they had to ditch in the sea, for it was their flying boots (fur-lined), flying-jacket (fur-lined) and fur-lined gloves that we were after: these were the first essentials, and we'd haul him over the side afterwards! Seriously, when one is searching for perhaps twelve hours in rain, hail or snow, something more than gumboots and a sweater was necessary; to peer over the top of the windscreen in driving snow at fifteen knots, looking for a yellow rubber dinghy, is not like watching the same thing on television.

Our second 'crash call' came at 2 am one morning. An aircraft had been seen to explode about ten miles south of the Isle of Wight: message 'to proceed at once to position and search'. We searched and searched, and suddenly picked up in our searchlight a parachute spinning across the sea. We closed in and saw a pilot attached. Catching a parachute and pulling the pilot aboard in a gale or wind in the middle of the night is a little difficult, but we recovered the pilot and found that he had no 'quick-release clip' on his parachute harness and had therefore been unable to release himself from his parachute. We could see no sign of life but one can never be sure, so artificial respiration was attempted for four hours until we finally gave up. In addition to this, for some odd reason all the lights in the boat suddenly went out and both engines stopped. We were then a mile off Dunnose Head, south of the Isle of Wight, with an onshore wind blowing.

With only torches to help them, the engineers and electrician traced the fault within ten minutes of possibly being blown ashore in the middle of the night. Returning to Portsmouth, we found that the pilot was an American, and details of his parachute without quick-release gear were passed to the Air Ministry. The man must have absorbed much sea water and drowned, although his 'Mae West' was fully inflated.

To most of the crew, life at sea was a little boring—crash-drills and rescue do not happen every day. It is not amusing for a man who has not been brought up with the sea to have to sit out in a rolling 60-foot launch for hours and days on end. Sea-sickness was common, but I seemed to enjoy the conditions. All was forgotten when we received a crash-call, however, for then everything is action— courses are plotted whilst the engines are warming up, call-signs checked, rough-weather clothing donned, and at fifteen knots we're off.

A typical crash-call was one that we received at six o'clock one summer evening. It was thought that an aircraft had been seen to explode somewhere between ten and twenty miles due south of the Needles (on the Isle of Wight). We immediately set off to a position fifteen miles south and started our square search. After three hours, nothing had been found. Suddenly, to the north of us, we saw a flare rise in the sky about five miles away. Taking a quick bearing, we set our course and in twenty minutes spotted our dinghy, with one occupant—an English fighter pilot. It transpired than he had seen us searching in the distance; he had seen our relatively big boat, while his dinghy was so small that we could not see him at five miles distance. He had had just one flare and had courageously held on to it until dusk, knowing that there was more chance of it being seen in the semi-darkness: his decision was right, for otherwise he might well have spent the night in the dinghy and never have been found at all.

Returning to base, I was told that there was a new fast boat allocated to me and that we were to go to Hampton on the Thames to commission it immediately. Handing over my old boat to another officer was like losing a very old and trusted friend, for she had carried me safely some thousands of miles over the sea and I had built up a great affection for her. However, collecting my crew, we went to London and thence to Hampton, to find a 60-foot Thornycroft HSL on the slipway ready to be launched. She had two Thornycroft 650 hp engines, 1000 gallons of high-octane fuel in self-sealing tanks (against stray bullets), two gun-turrets (revolving) containing twin Browning guns—this was just what I wanted. Accommodation was a wheelhouse and a bridge above; below, there was a large sick-bay, a sleeping-cabin for me to starboard, and the radio-cabin opposite. Mounted on the deck, aft, was an Oerlikon gun; scrambling-nets for survivors to clamber up, port and starboard, completed the boat.

Taking over a new craft entails much work, for in wartime craft were built quickly and it paid to check the workmanship of the hull, steering and all under-water units such as cutlass-bearings, propellor shafts and propellors, water inlets and outlets. Aboard ship, the guns, radio, engines, batteries, toilets, fresh-water system—everything had to be checked and rechecked. A week passed before we left; underway the next morning, we cruised past Westminster Bridge and Southend, out to sea through the same graveyard of ships. We stopped at Dover for the night—very much a wartime Dover with the occasional big shells dropping, fired from the enemy-occupied French coast just a few miles away. Next morning, one fast run and we were back at the Rescue Base in Cowes.

The next day we were once more on rendez-vous off the 'Nab Tower'. That evening, at 20.00 hours, we received a crash call to a position off Selsey Bill. Fog had descended, and it was like searching for the proverbial needle in a haystack. All night we searched, stopping every five minutes and cutting the engines to listen for any sound of whistles (which were supplied as part of the survival-kit issued to aircraft crew). At first light we received a radio call to go to a position twenty miles due south, Selsey Bill.

In half an hour we found them—the whole of an American Fortress crew in one large yellow rubber dinghy—eleven men. One of the men was cranking a hand radio-set, connected to a balloon high up in the air by a fine wire and emitting distress-calls. We came alongside the dinghy and they scrambled up the nets like ants and devoured a breakfast of bacon and eggs and everything edible that we had on board. They soon recovered and generously gave us their flying-boots for the crew.

Next day we had to remain on the slipway to check a faulty propellor. In the dark we had a full-speed encounter with a large rope fender that had broken away from a big Naval vessel, resulting in our shaft being slightly bent. In daylight one always keeps a good eye open to floating objects, for they can do great damage at high speed; at night, of course, you cannot see these things—you just hope that you do not hit one.

A week later we were once more in operation, on rendez-vous off the south of the Island at 06.00 hours, covering a strike of our aircraft over France. With the early-morning mist rising off the sea and lifting over the cliffs of Ventnor just touched by the sunrise, the scene was wondrous. In close company was a fishing boat whose crew were just finishing hauling up their trawls from the night's fishing. Here was a chance for some fresh fish: we closed on them and after a tot of rum they generously handed over a large bucket of magnificent plaice. To be able to remember an incident like that, thirty years after, makes me realise how delicious those fish were. We trimmed off their fins and tails and fried them for our breakfast: I cannot attempt to describe the flavour of those plaice, fresh from the sea at seven in the morning—exquisite.

It was a little later, whilst we were 'listening out' on the R/T that a voice suddenly came across—'Spitfire in sea, position, etc, etc.' This was unusual, for every message—even a very urgent one—always had a secret prefix; and after much heart searching we decided to ignore it. It was as well, for we were informed later that it was transmitted by a German E-boat that had endeavoured to lure any nearby vessel to that position. The E-boats also had a nasty habit, when there was fog in the Channel, of tying up to the one and only navigation buoy off Lyme Bay at night: when convoys passed this area, a small blip showed on their radar, apparently showing the position of the buoy. The E-boat then sprang to life at the appropriate moment and attacked the convoy, afterwards beating a swift retreat across the Channel into the night.

Later that day, we were joined by a naval MASB (Motor Anti-Submarine Boat), a boat about the same size as ourselves and with approximately the same speed; and from then on we searched in tandem. This MASB carried four depth-charges and one morning decided that it was time he tested one. The skipper called up the Naval Officer in charge of the Isle of Wight for permission to drop a depth charge. His answer was kindly: 'Yes, drop it in St Catherine's Deeps, there are more fish there!' We duly did this, keeping well away from the huge explosion. The variety of fish brought to the surface was incredible—nearly all sea-bass, and I also remember a huge conger eel, five feet long and a foot in diameter. Now, one doesn't play games with a conger eel—of any size—and this one was only stunned; its head was immediately cut off and the fish gutted.

That evening the Naval Officer had twelve large bass for his Officers' Mess, and we and the MASB sat down to our evening meal. At about nine o'clock we heard the sound of enemy bombers. Rushing on deck alongside the pier at Seaview, we could see that Portsmouth was being badly bombed: the anti-aircraft fire was terrific—so much so that the German bombers were dropping their bombs short of Portsmouth, around us and the area of the two Sea Forts at Spithead; flares were lighting up the whole scene between Portsmouth and the Isle of Wight. This went on until 02.00 hours, and then we retired to our bunks. At 06.00 hours we received a crash-call to a position ten miles off Cherbourg on the French German-occupied coast. On no account were we to search inside the ten-mile range. Two big dinghies had been seen by returning English fighters, and the Royal Air Force wanted the survivors to be captured, eleven in all, and brought back for interrogation, for a German aircraft containing eleven men was unheard of.

At 06.15 we and the MASB raced across the Channel. Everything had been stowed away for the weather was rough—every moveable object was put on the floor of the cabin (where it all finishes anyhow), eggs were put in a large tin of rice (a good tip here for the cruising man), and large mugs of tea were made continuously on the way over. At 09.00 hours, a Spitfire approached us, 'waggled it wings' to convey that there was something

ahead, turned, gave us his course, and then turned for home. We arrived on position and could see two objects floating on the water in the distance. Closing in we saw two naval 'Carley Floats', survivor floats carried by both foreign and British Navies. One of the floats held six German sailors, the other five. The MASB took five of the Germans, put them on his foredeck, and set course for Portsmouth. We took the other six and put them down in the sick-bay in the charge of a sergeant and three of the crew, with one sten gun between us. Fortunately they were in no state to cause any disturbance, most of them appearing to be shell-shocked.

We found out later that they were the crew of a German E-boat which had been cruising up the Channel. In the dark a French destroyer had picked the E-boat up on its radar, closed in, suddenly trained their searchlights on it and blown it out of the water in one fusillade of shell-fire.

Several weeks passed in making rendez-vous in the Channel, covering strikes by our aircraft on the French Coast. One day the Nab Tower flashed us a message: 'Proceed to position 55 miles, 185 degrees Nab.' Setting course on our grid compass, with the electric log at 0, compensating for the westerly tide at one and a half knots, we adjusted our speed to 27 knots and set off in company with another RAF launch.

Arriving at our estimated position, both boats then started the usual square search, going in opposite directions. The weather was very rough and getting worse. After four hours of searching as daylight vanished we suddenly had a radio message to return to base because of gale conditions. We were naturally furious, for, whilst it was no weather for us to be out in, it was considerably worse for the dinghy that we were searching for. The next day we were weather-bound in harbour, and had to content ourselves with working out the estimated position that we thought the dinghy must have arrived at with the east and west tides and a westerly gale. Next day the gale was abating, so HSL 192 and my HSL 198 set off again to the new estimated position of the dinghy that we had plotted on our charts. After four hours we both spotted the dinghy. To our surprise, the pilot was just strong enough to climb up the scrambling-net of HSL 192. He was a Mosquito pilot and his navigator had been lost. Whilst he was being helped up the scrambling-net we were keeping an eye on the enemy coast at Cherbourg which was about eight miles away, and also keeping a look out for enemy fighters. Three shells landed—one to port, one to starboard, and one astern: nice grouping! . . . We both made off fast on a zig-zag course, endeavouring to 'make smoke' to cover our exit. The pilot was taken back to Seaview and placed in the Naval sick-bay, where he gently recovered from the three days in gale-force conditions in a rubber dinghy. The RAF learnt many things from this pilot—how to survive at sea, good and bad points about rubber dinghies, and so on.

◀
Saro Princess flying boat

Andes

73

There is an interesting sequel to this rescue. About fifteen years later, HRH Prince Philip was paying a visit to the Island Sailing Club at Cowes together with his Equerry, Wing Commander Peter Horsley. Meeting in the club, Wing Commander Horsley noticed that I by chance was wearing an Air-Sea Rescue tie, and he by chance was wearing a 'Goldfish Tie'—a tie only available to pilots who had 'ditched' in the sea in wartime and lived to tell the tale.

After a few minutes we both realised that he was the pilot we had picked up with HSL 192 off Cherbourg—what a reunion then took place! I have since written to Sir Peter Horsley, as he now is, and here is his side of the story.

'The details of my struggle with Father Neptune are still vivid. I remember the incident as a very personal encounter, where I was to survive against the sea which was equally determined to engulf me. I made many mistakes which nearly cost me my life, but basically it was luck, physical fitness and my RAF training which contributed most to my survival. The worst mistake I made was, at one stage, to desert the dinghy, which I seemed incapable of steering, and try and swim to the shore about ten miles distant. Fortunately after fifty metres or so I came to my senses and just found enough strength to return; but it sapped all my strength badly. There were many poor design features in the dinghy, apart from its size which was excruciatingly small, the worst being the ease with which it turned turtle. Since the sea was rough, it did this many times, which was followed by the inevitable struggle to right it and get up into it again. These sequences more than anything took their toll and led me to my ultimate surrender on the third day. There was one funny part—I had decided that to keep my health going I should perform my usual 'toilets' in the dinghy, which became too foul to put up with. So I tried to remedy this by putting my bottom over the side of the dinghy, which resulted in my doing a backward flip into the water with my trousers round my ankles. I only wished it could have been filmed as it was worthy of the best of the Charlie Chaplin antics.

There were also some strange aspects to the experience which I believe are not unknown in moments of extreme mental and physical stress. For example, I seemed to float away from my body and I remember clearly looking down on myself in the sea. Towards the end I began to drift away into another world of incredible peacefulness made up of scenes and people (Douglas Bader wrote about the same experience when he was close to death after the amputation of his legs), and all the time I knew I had to fight my way back to reality—the sea. On the third day, I did give myself up to this peacefulness and thereafter remember little. F/Lt Newman on HSL 192 did say that I was out of my dinghy with my Mae West on (*author's note:*—this is true, the dinghy was close by). I am not a particularly religious person but I felt, in such an isolated position where final drowning appeared inevitable, that there were other forces at work.

'The whole episode left me with a very philosophical view of life, in that while other people do tend to take life's problems and set-backs seriously, I have viewed them less so, in the knowledge that the important thing is life itself; therefore I have become more inclined to live each day for itself' (Sir Peter Horsley retired from the Royal Air Force in 1976).

If the reader has formed the impression that these rescues were cold and factual, of course they were not. To be separated from the sea by a piece of thin rubber dinghy, even for four hours in the English Channel, hoping that one is found, is bound to make a man's thoughts chaotic. Our task was to save people from possible drowning knowing that each minute of delay was vital; at the first sight of a dinghy with a live occupant one thanked God for one's eyesight and determination to beat the sea at its own game. One sight, however, remains in my memory—that of a young (he looked seventeen) navigator in Air Force blue curled up in a tiny dinghy, as if he was just about to be born into this world. We thought he might be asleep, but he had passed into the next world; his mother will know that he was lifted tenderly out of his little cocoon and returned to his squadron to be given a burial by his brother aircrew.

Many weeks passed on rendez-vous, for there were continuous strikes by our aircraft across the Channel. Searching at 25 to 30 knots on a rough sea is like racing over concrete blocks at every two seconds—each wave feels solid, your knees flex, you wait for the next and the next and the next, sometimes for six hours; your eyes water over the edge of the flying bridge with the continual rush of cold air and the strain of searching for a tiny rubber dinghy six feet long (or a half-submerged log of timber); goggles are useless with the fine salt spray; and the gunners in their turrets are continually circling and endeavouring not to be sea-sick. The engineers down below, strapped to their seats just one foot away from their screaming engines, are alert for a sudden quick fall in oil pressure which would ruin an engine in seconds.

On one occasion as we approached approximately fifteen miles from the enemy-occupied French coast, the gunners shouted and pointed ahead—a cloud of about sixty fighters were headed for us, skimming the wave-tops. Christ! In seconds they were upon us—and gone—Spitfires returning from a 'strike'. We cursed the Air Ministry for not informing us of the strike, for the fighters could have been enemy and we could have shot at them. We received the recall to base. . . .

When you step ashore you cannot walk, your knees are like water, and your liver, kidneys and other movable parts of your body feel out of place.

The Normandy Invasion

There was an air of expectancy in the three Services in May 1944. Continual daily strikes were being made across the Channel, keeping us busy on rendez-vous at sea; no enemy aircraft were seen in our area; and the Solent was literally packed with Naval vessels of all descriptions—one felt that one could literally have walked across from the Isle of Wight to Southampton on the decks of ships. Commando ships (small liners) that had been converted for assault bristled with rockets and guns; tank landing-craft, destroyers, minelayers, ships that had never been seen before towing huge *caissons* of concrete, later to be called 'Mulberry Harbour'. On the south of the island, work of a secret nature was being done with huge pipe-laying vessels in attendance preparing the vast tube that was eventually to straddle the bottom of the Channel, supplying fuel under the code name of– Pluto.

The Isle of Wight became a very restricted area. Loose talk and telephone conversations to the mainland were kept under rigorous surveillance: I remember one farmer who had telephoned to the mainland who was apprehended for having said 'The commandos are ready'—it later turned out that what he had said was 'The tomatoes are ready'!

Leviathan

On the evening of 5 June we made rendez-vous ten miles south of the island; towards the west, with a visibility of twenty miles, we could see what appeared to be thousands of tiny stars in a huge bunch. It was the last rays of the setting sun below the horizon, reflecting on thousands of barrage balloons flown by the ships of the Normandy Invasion—it had begun!

All that night and the next day we were surrounded by thousands of

ships and craft of all types—all trekking south, and there was no need to
have a compass aboard. Great rocket-carrying craft, battleships, cruisers
and fast destroyers of the allied navies. . . . We saw a destroyer at full
speed suddenly make a 90-degree turn to port to avoid a mine. It was an
awe-inspiring sight, for she laid over to starboard at more than 45 degrees,
the narrow metal deck aft suddenly becoming a boiling torrent of rushing
water, fatal to any seaman who happened to be on the deck—he would
have gone in a flash. One latecomer, a tiny personnel landing-craft with
twenty commandos aboard, had broken down. We closed on him, he
restarted, asked us which way was France, we pointed, and he was gone.
On rendez-vous in the middle of the Channel, we did not have a single
crash-call during the whole invasion. The Air Force had fought the enemy
over French soil and any damaged aircraft managed to land behind our
lines—our work was finished in the English Channel.

Looking back over that period one thinks of all the men who had to
become seamen in so short a time—and how one automatically recognises
a man used to the sea. Little things tell a big story: you will never see a
seaman standing on deck with a foot in the middle of a coil of rope, or
standing astride a straining wire or rope (he has too much respect for his
manhood—once is enough). I once saw one vessel towing another and a
man standing directly in line with the tow-rope which was under terrific
tension. The rope broke and whipped back like a coiled spring, striking the
man on the deck. He was lucky not to lose an eye—or both eyes. One can
only learn by experience, I suppose.

However, three weeks later I received a posting to, of all places, the
Shetland Isles again, this time to a tiny fishing vilage called Scalloway on
the west coast; there I was to take over a 73-foot Vosper high-speed
launch. She had three petrol engines, and her armament consisted of two
sets of twin Browning machine guns in revolving turrets and an Oerlikon
gun aft. Her hull was round-bilged from the bow, flattening off about
fifteen feet from the stern, and she had a speed of about 35 knots. The
engines all turned the propellors in the same direction—to starboard, due
no doubt to the shortage of equipment in wartime. The result was that
when the craft accelerated ahead, it took a list of about fifteen degrees to
port; combined with a strong wind abeam on the 'wrong' side this added
another fifteen degrees to the list (and there was plenty of wind in this
area), making a list to port of thirty degrees—in fact the craft behaved
more like a submarine than a surface craft.

It was about this time that a rumour spread that the *Queen Mary*,
operating in high northern waters, had under bad weather conditions, cut
clean through *HMS Curacao*, a cruiser, and merely reported in the log that
she had struck a particularly heavy sea with very slight bow damage, not
realising that she had struck another craft. It seems incredible, and yet

possible with these great ships travelling at speed. No doubt Naval records will prove or disprove the story.

Our task in this area was to operate between the Shetlands and Norway—a rough, nasty area for small boats as the public now know with all the news of oil-rigs that comes through today. Norway was still occupied by the enemy, and raids were operating both at sea and by aircraft. A Catalina seaplane, crewed by a Norwegian squadron, made a secret weekly visit to a Norwegian fjord, picked up and replaced vital personnel and documents, without the enemy ever knowing.

It was about this time that the 'airborne lifeboat' was being used with success. There were two types, 23 feet and 30 feet long, shaped like a long canoe, unsinkable, to be carried under the body of a bomber aircraft. The Hudson aircraft was first used, then the Wellington, and finally the Lancaster bomber. It was a masterpiece of thinking.

The idea was that as soon as an aircraft had been shot down near enemy coast or long distances from the English coast this bomber would proceed to the rubber dinghy position and drop the airborne lifeboat on three parachutes. As the lifeboat hit the water, three rockets automatically fired, throwing three sea-drogues to hold the lifeboat in position and stop it from blowing away from the survivors in the rubber dinghy. The lifeboat was fully equipped with engine, petrol, water, food, flares, distress radio, sails, mast and oars. On the earlier models, the engine was hand started, but after a survivor had complained that his hands were too frozen to crank the engine a small accumulator was added for instant starting. The whole idea was a success, and entire crews of Fortresses and the bigger bombers were rescued by these craft.

Our high-speed launches were to proceed and find these airborne lifeboats, pick up the survivors, and head back to base fast. We came upon one such craft, gently sailing (with additional engine) from the Norwegian coast, for all the world as if the occupants were out for a sail for the day and enjoying it! We picked them off, but unfortunately had to sink the craft as we could not tow it at high speed and enemy aircraft were about. This was just as well, for about sixty miles north-east of Shetland a roaring north-westerly gale hit us on the starboard quarter.

Now, a gale in that area is normally 'beyond the common experience of man', especially in a small boat—in plain English, the boat was a bastard. With huge following seas, we 'broached to' to starboard every five minutes. The port gunner in his gun turret looked more like a submariner and had to come inboard. All spare warps were towed astern, drogues and sea-anchors dragged astern, engines adjusted, but nothing would stop that continual broaching. I pay tribute to our two engineers who were strapped to their seats below in the engine room in front of their engines, at full throttle, the hatches battened down. With the heat and noise of these engines and the continual broaching of the launch, they must have thought that they were in Dante's inferno. On deck, the seas were building high astern and then sweeping the decks, and the bow surging into the preceding wave followed by the inevitable broaching; it was nearing dusk; and for common safety we decided to enter the northern entrance of Lerwick on the east side of Shetland. The entrance is bad as there is an ugly, huge, flat rock in the narrow entrance which is normally awash and can be seen; but with the light there was that day, it was invisible. With one huge following sea I think we must have been carried over it, for within seconds we were in shelter. Everyone I think once in their lifetime experiences genuine fear, and I must say that I thought our time had come once or twice on the trip back to Lerwick. That area of sea is cold, hard and pitiless in winter.

However, as I have said before, one forgets the bad times and only remembers the good. Returning to Scalloway on the west coast, life eased and we could enjoy the rugged grandeur of the coast. I bought a Shetland Dory with a dipping lug and spent hours sailing in and out of the bays. The fishing was incredible. I am no fisherman, but I could not help catching fish there. Halibut, tuna and cod abound; haddock, with that lifelike 'thumbprint' of St David on their bodies, were in plentiful supply; and once or twice I had to cut the thick codline which I used as fishing line, for I had something down below on the hook so heavy that it was pulling the dory ahead.

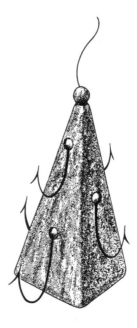

There are many seals in this area. As you walked along the sandy beaches, these almost human animals would swim gently alongside—if they could have spoken, I am sure they would have done.

Daylight, in winter, is restricted to about six hours, and the life is hard and rugged. Fishing is the main support of the people of Scalloway. One particular form of hook is called a 'murderer' (as in the diagram). It is well-named, for if you drop this appliance deep into the water and lift it up and down sharply, the hooks bite into the fish at all angles and you pull up six fish at a time. In one day's fishing by myself, I caught four hundred fish and was knee deep in them in the dory. I sailed back into the harbour and gave the fish to the local fishermen.

It was now March, 1945, and the hard winter in the Shetlands was beginning to tell on my physical condition. I thought it was time to shelve the responsibility of having eleven men out at sea, and requested a posting ashore. This was granted, and I was sent to HQ16 Group Coastal Command in Gillingham, Kent. Two months later, the war in Europe ended and I applied for demobilisation. The medical team who examined me included by coincidence, the medical officer who had first examined me on joining the Forces. He said it was about time that he and I came out, so we gave each other our 'bowler hat' and that was that.

Reflecting on life in the Services, my vivid memories are all of the sea. In the midst of all the strife and destruction, when everybody was being taught to destroy lives, we at least were trying to save them. I recall the calm of the English Channel when sometimes a ripple could not be seen between the English and French coasts. I remember the seas off Norway and Shetland where it blows with such violence and the seas are so tempestuous that the seagulls begin to look like vultures. . . .

I also remember the 'new boy' of the crew who had learnt the correct way of throwing a bucket overboard on a rope's end to pick up seawater to wash the deck. Unfortunately we were travelling at thirty knots at the time—he couldn't have gone overboard quicker. Fortunately he had both his legs outside the safety lines otherwise his voice would now be two octaves higher.

Two incidents are worth recording, which could be a warning to all people who go on the sea. In the first, one of our HSL's had just finished refuelling with a thousand gallons of high-octane fuel, in harbour, and the engineer disappeared down his engine-hatch to check. A split second later there was a loud explosion and he jetted out, on fire, fortunately going straight into the water. It was thought he must have had a metal stud on his shoe which sparked with the metal ladder; we never knew, for his shoes were never found again.

The other incident took place off the eastern end of the Isle of Wight. The 'gate' (an anti-submarine net stretched between the two forts) was closed for the night, and we were attached to a French submarine-chaser anchored off Bembridge by four warps and the anchor chain to its stern. At midnight, with no warning, a gale sprang up from the south-east. In the ensuing seas the two 'Sampson Posts' (oak and 6″ thick) snapped off at deck-level and our warps were gone. The French sub-chaser had fixed our anchor-chain with riding turns and couldn't release it; we had no cold chisel to break our chain and had to reverse at full speed to break the chain in the high seas, which we finally managed (and in the process I lost two of my fingers). Then we had to steam for eight hours gently into the gale, first on one engine and then on the other to prevent oiling up. Here is a warning always to carry a cold chisel and hammer aboard.

Of course I shall never forget the Shetland Isles—the kindly people; the same old gull lifting off the same rock, searching for a morsel of food from our boat; the utter peace and quiet of Scalloway, broken by the 'thump' of the big gulls as they land on the tin roof of the sleeping huts; and finally—Stranraer, where I had my first air-sea rescue course, with the small isle of Ailsa Craig a few miles off and the comment by the locals for the weather forecast: 'If you can see Ailsa Craig, it's going to rain; and if you can't see it, it is raining.' It was also in Shetland that I heard the alleged true story of a telegram that Sir Winston Churchill was supposed to have sent to Sir Andrew Cunningham when, after destroying most of the Italian Fleet in the Mediterranean, he had been knighted for the second time: 'Twice a night at your age—I'm surprised.'

Tovarisch, bound from Plymouth to New York, Operation Sail, 1976

▶

Keith Beken at work

Back to Civilian Life

Returning to civilian life in 1945 at the age of thirty-one, having had six years sliced out of one's life working for an employer (the Government), life was inevitably unsettling. After years of the company of men only, to come back to one's home town where everybody one knew seemed to have disappeared. . . . With the thought of a further fifty years ahead of me, I was determined to spend as many of them as possible in contact with the sea. I had touched the past and must prepare for the future and use the sea as much as possible—watch it, listen and feel the heartbeats of the world which sails on it: I had already become dedicated to it without knowing it.

My father, in his innate wisdom and kindness to people, had determined at an early age to make his photographs available at a price accessible not only to wealthy yachtsmen but also to all the enthusiastic youngsters taking to the sea in small boats. They could be bought by everybody, and as a result they came to be seen all over the world. I was determined to carry on this principle, but with one difference: the chemist business had always financed the photographic section, and I was determined that our marine photography should stand on its own two feet.

I recall, now with amusement but at that time with anger, one of our first commissions to photograph a yacht for a lady owner. Having spent a great deal of time and care in photographing the yacht, and in processing and printing the six photographs, the lady came in the next week to see the results. After studying the photographs with great care, she said, 'Yes, very nice, but I don't want them as I see that I am wearing my glasses.' What does one say to that, apart from 'Madam, I photograph bloody yachts not bloody women'? It was also around the same time that I

Prince Philip at the helm, Uffa Fox crewing, in *Coweslip*, Uffa Fox's Flying Fifteen design noticed, when I was about to take a photograph of a sailing cruiser on my own initiative, the unusually attractive young lady companion who was sitting in the cockpit swiftly rose and disappeared into the cabin. After this had happened a number of times, I came to a certain conclusion—and henceforth took plenty of time to signify that I was about to take a photograph—Ah well!

When I had entered the air-sea rescue service during the war, I had made a habit of carrying a small notebook in my pocket and entering in this book any unusual and interesting event, design or idea that I had seen. It is a thing that any young fellow, with a job that brings him in contact with interesting people, books, designs, etc, must do, especially if he moves around the world at all. The pocket-book should be fixed-leaf, so that those original notes and dreams remain there forever and are not torn out to disappear into the maelstrom of life.

Turning over the pages, I found some ideas about a new camera that I had noted and I immediately started to design a new version, a Mark II of the original camera with some refinements. Always our 'enemy' is movement of the boat and therefore of the camera. A new 'Compur' shutter had become available, and was, fortunately, practically the same diameter as the lenses of the old camera. The brass mount of the lens was only 1½ mm thick, and to rethread this mount to fit the mount of the shutter was an extremely delicate job; but with the aid of a gunsmith's lathe it was accomplished and fitted to the shutter, which had a speed of 1/500th of a second.

Our original launch reappeared from its hiding place, was overhauled, and was put on a mooring in the harbour opposite our house so that it could be permanently in view. This was useful since, when a gale was forecast, we could immediately row out to her and take her up the river, safe from a north-easterly gale. It took a year or two after the war for yachts once more to make their reappearance, and the country was of course short of materials for new hulls, spars and engines, etc, but it was not long before all the old yachts started to reappear from their laying-up quarters—those, that is, that had not been commandeered for the war effort. Fife of Scotland, Camper and Nicholson and Vospers of England— all designers and builders slowly started to develop new craft, as their contracts for Naval vessels ceased. New yards were being formed and yachtsmen were dying to get afloat, motor cars were in short supply, and people naturally turned to the sea for relaxation.

The yard of Uffa Fox Ltd was developing and building the international 14-foot dinghy class. He completely revolutionised sailing dinghies by designing the first-ever dinghy that could plane. It was really a break-through in design and type of building, and he took every cup there was available to be won. Each dinghy he built was faster than the previous one, and this of course presented us with new problems in photographing them, for at one moment they are travelling at perhaps five knots and the next at fifteen knots. One had to use one's own knowledge of dinghy racing to estimate just when they were about to get up and plane. I knew no man at that time who could sail a dinghy as Uffa could. He seemed to sail it without effort, never really seeming to 'sit out' the dinghy; but with deft use of rudder and sails he was always up to weather and in the lead. Uffa and his crew sailed a dinghy across the Channel to France, racing at all the regattas along the coast, put all the cups in the bottom of the dinghy, and sailed back to the Isle of Wight. They took 27 hours to sail across to Le Havre and 37 hours to return to Cowes. In his 'Avenger' dinghy, out of 57 races he obtained 52 firsts, 2 seconds and 3 thirds. I had the opportunity of racing with Uffa one day off Yarmouth (IOW) in the six-metre class. The start was in a practically flat calm condition, with just enough air to fill the sails. We had a bad start, lying seventh out of nine starters, all in close company. Uffa immediately started to tell 'risque' stories within earshot of the other helmsmen, and they were listened to with rapt attention—but by the time we were at the first mark, we were in the lead. As Uffa said, 'If you can't do anything else, at least distract the enemy.'

Uffa was a great friend, and completely irrepressible. It was he who conceived the idea of playing cricket in the middle of the Solent. In September each year, at the time of the Equinox, the 'Brambles Bank' between Cowes and Southampton is visible about ten centimetres high at extreme low tide, on one day only, for about one hour. VIPs from the Isle of Wight, including the Governor of Parkhurst Prison and the Governor of Osborne House—six people in all—were challenged to play cricket on the Bank, against six Cowes people. The navigator of a passing Dutch liner was horrified to see twelve men playing cricket on what (according to his chart) should have been sea: he probably thought he had missed a turning and was heading up the Thames for Lord's Cricket Ground.

In later years, Uffa designed his 'Flying Fifteen', the keels of which could be unbolted so that, with the hull on the top of a car, it could easily be transported to regattas along the coast: They were an instant success, and the Island Sailing Club at Cowes presented one to HRH Prince Philip; with Uffa as crew, it was raced year after year. I had one for many years and it gave me some enjoyable racing. The rigging was simple and effective—just mainstays, fore and backstay, without runners—and one could race in the roughest of weather, rising quickly and easily, and planing like a dinghy. It had been described as 'the boat for the older man', as it was not necessary to sit it out with trapazes. However, judging from the amount of sea-water that flew about, I now think it is not so much for older people as for active people of whatever age.

On the subject of small boat racing, I have recently read an article by

Jack Knights, the eminent helmsman and journalist. He says: 'He was plunging headlong, ricochetting, sliding at impossible angles, yet he retained his precarious balance with one part of his mind coolly planning how to negotiate the obstacles which lay ahead.' He is talking about Franz Klammer, the Olympic ski-champion, and goes on to say: 'There is one skill that does compare (with the downhill ski-racer) and that is driving an overpressed racing dinghy downwind in a seaway; the human, in much the same way, has his hands as well as legs, eyes and nerves more than full in defying the normal natural laws. . . .' How true this statement of Jack Knight's is: he's done it, I've done it, and many dedicated dinghy-sailors have done it—waited for the Force 5 just for the sheer joy, and to hell with the long beat back. What greater excitment does one want than to be in the lead (in the 'hot seat') of your class, on a hair-raising run with the tiller feeling solid on the plane and all your competitors praying for you to capsize.

Beken & Son, Cowes

I was married in 1947, and the next year we were blessed with a son, and three years later another son. Now I was doubly blessed. Like all children who live by the sea, they fell in it, nearly drowned in it, swam in it, were out too late on it, had boats looking for them on it when they should have been in bed—in fact they behaved like any normal kids, in order to become proficient on the sea.

With the enthusiasm I had for sailing, I took the opportunity to sail and race bigger yachts, for in this way I could not only enjoy but also study and appreciate their behaviour under all conditions and formulate the angles at which they looked their best. A yawl or ketch, for instance, with mizzen, main, and jibs plus a spinnaker and mizzen staysail, is much more photogenic than a sloop with mainsail and big genoa: there are more sails and therefore more curves to compose your picture, and foreknowledge of when these sails will be set is absolutely essential.

The first cross-channel race to start after the war was a race from Cowes to Dinard, and I had the opportunity of crewing on a yacht called *Ragna*, a Class 2 Ocean Racer. She had been bought as a speculation, for resale, by a gentleman who knew little about racing; Henry Rooke was the skipper, the two Ponsonby brothers, 'Cocoa' Fry and two or three others were crew. The course was first to a mark off Brixham, Devon, to avoid a minefield west of the Isle of Wight, and thence across to Dinard in France. We left Cowes at 18.00 hours on Friday with a moderate westerly blowing; just outside the Needles we received a gale-warning—westerly. Off Portland Bill the gale struck. I remember little of that night because of the violent motion of *Ragna*, so completely different from the air-sea rescue launches in which I had never been seasick in four years. This time I really was seasick. I retired to the floor of the cabin and hoped the craft would sink and put me out of my misery; those people who have had a similar experience will know what I mean. I remember sea-boots walking over me as sails were dragged from the cockpit forward. I remember seeing also the owner of *Ragna,* with a big mug tucked under his chin, lying across the port bunk being terribly seasick—and seeing him thrown across into the starboard bunk complete with mug. I remember also surfacing at 06.00 hours in the morning, imagining that we must be off Brixham and finding that we were still off Portland. It took another ten hours for us to beat into Brixham, where the owner of *Ragna* and I both left the yacht as we had to return to our various businesses and were in any case not in a completely fit state to continue across the Channel in the gale. I recovered, of course—one always does—and after a few weeks one does exactly the same thing again: it must be masochism. It wasn't until the next year that I had the chance of racing again, this time to Cherbourg, on a 10-ton loose-footed main-gaff cutter, designed by Albert Strange. Again the race was a bit bumpy overnight, but with the loose-footed main she was comfortable. About halfway across, around 02.00 hours, the Calor Gas bottle worked itself loose from its seating, fell and hit the owner of the boat, a doctor, in the chest, cracking two ribs. Fortunately we had a medical crew aboard, another doctor, so we strapped up the owner and on arrival at Cherbourg managed to get him into the sick-bay of the *Queen Mary* which was lying alongside the quay and sailing to Southampton that evening. When the *Queen Mary* was halfway across the Channel, the ship's doctor telephoned to the doctor's partner ashore, about midnight, the conversation being somewhat like this:

RMS *Queen Mary*   'Hello, this is Queen Mary.'
Answer   'Yes, and this is King George'
     (puts telephone down).

2nd telephone call:
RMS *Queen Mary*   'Hello, this is Queen Mary.'
Answer   'And this is the Kaiser and I don't want to buy a
     battleship' (puts the telephone down).

Ah well, he can be forgiven; we have all given and received 'funny' phone calls in our youth at midnight.

By 1950, this was the pattern into which my life was evolving. Photographing was becoming an obsession, as well as a necessity. Unfortunately I had the wrong hobby, for to sail and photograph other yachts at the same time was impossible, most yachting being done at weekends, as was racing, of course. Inevitably I had to refuse invitations to race, and photography became a full-time job. My racing had to confine itself to evenings in the summer.

An interesting permanent contract was to photograph most of the great liners which sailed into and out of Southampton, across the world's

▶
Eagle

▶
Gitana

seas—the Royal Mail fleet, the Pacific and Orient Line, and of course the Cunard Line. We were asked to photograph the *Andes* of the Royal Mail and eliminate all smoke from the funnels. Now, this was easier said than done, for to retouch all smoke from the negatives was an impossibility. The captain was asked if he could not 'cut smoke' for five minutes as he went past us. Next day as he sailed past we signalled, and magically the funnels ceased to emit smoke. How he did this I never knew—I imagined he had a Red Indian in the funnel with a blanket making his 'smoke signals'—however, it was completely successful.

These great ships in those days had no stabilisers, and I well remember the *Leviathan,* a great three-funnelled ship, arriving from a gale in the Channel with a long, slow roll from side to side, rolling round Calshot Light Vessel and up Southampton Water and even alongside the quay, which was always dangerous with possible damage to ship and quay. Today you never see that at all—one great advance in the comfort of passengers. Every ship has just one angle at which it looks its best, and it is necessary to be able to spot this almost at once; for, with our launch only being able to motor at a maximum of eight knots and the liner approaching at perhaps fifteen knots, I had only one chance of photographing at this angle. This 'best' angle depends upon so many things—the shape of the bow, the shape and number of funnels, the shape of the stern, and not least the angle of the sun upon the ship as a whole. Normally a ship looks its best when the sun is ahead of it. The shadows are right, but this of course depends upon whether the ship is steaming into the sun, which does not always happen. It depends upon the time of day and the course of the ship, as you cannot ask a liner to turn around and approach the sun when she is on her way to South Africa. This 'best angle' is determined, I think, only by instinct and an inherent gift for 'composition', even using a cloud to balance a picture. Many times you look at paintings, and perhaps one will appeal more than all the others: usually it is because of the composition of subjects that the artist has used—it is literally 'easy on the eye'.

Whenever the maiden voyage of one of these great ships occurs, with the waving crowds ashore and afloat, the bands playing, the blasting of the ship's siren, etc, it never fails to remind me of the maiden voyage of the *Titanic,* that huge four-funnelled unsinkable pride of the Cunard Fleet which sank so tragically a few days out at sea after hitting an iceberg, with practically total loss of crew and passengers. The photograph of her taken on that maiden (and only) voyage must be the last ever taken of her.

◄

Sundowner

In the memoirs of my father, I came across the following:

Whilst I was out in the Solent taking photographs, I noticed the battleship HMS *Hawke* approaching from the west; at the same time the liner *Olympic* was approaching from Southampton Water. The two ships seemed to me to be inevitably on a collision course; the *Olympic* turned to port to the eastward, when suddenly the HMS *Hawke* also turned to port and hit the *Olympic* in the starboard quarter—a huge hole was torn in the *Olympic* and the *Hawke* listed so heavily starboard that I thought she was going to capsize; her bows were completely smashed. I took two photographs, the last I had; later I met the captain and officers of the *Olympic* at the Law Courts in London and was surprised at the extraordinary verdict, exonerating the captain of the *Hawke*. It was a few weeks after this that the *Titanic* passed us on her ill-fated voyage. Her sinking was a great shock to me personally, for the captain and officers were those of the *Olympic*, whom I had met at the Law Courts and who had been promoted to the *Titanic*.

Of all the liners that we have photographed, I think the RMS *Andes* was the most beautifully proportioned, looking more like a large private motor yacht from any angle. The *Queen Mary* I think was the most impressive, and I had the good fortune to see the *Queen Elizabeth I* in the Clyde, painted battleship grey since she was being used to transport troops from America to England, defeating the U-boats with her speed of 30 knots. One photograph that I would always like to have taken is that of a modern ocean liner crossing the Atlantic at 30 knots. It must be an impressive sight for it is impressive enough to see a destroyer, which is so much smaller, at the same speed.

Launching-ceremonies, of which there have been many both large and small, are in their own way emotional events. With a big ship, it is as if a small town were being launched, with the hundreds of cabins, a veritable power-station of electricity, shops, restaurants, swimming-pools—everything that a town possesses.

The VIP lady stands on her platform, pulls the lever—'I name this ship "Queen Mary". . . . God bless her and all who sail in her'—the champagne bottle explodes on the stern, the dragging chains rattle and roar as she slides down the ways, a huge cloud of dust from either side rises in the air, cheers come from two thousand men lining the slipway, and gracefully the ship takes the water on her first step of her life. It is always remarkable to me (not being a designer) to see a boat, particularly a yacht, when launched, float exactly to her marks, so that when loaded with all the requisite sails and the hundred-and-one things that go into a yacht, she floats exactly to her waterline, as drawn on her original plans (perhaps some designers have their 'tongues in their cheeks' at this statement?).

In those days, to photograph the ceremony of a launching, I was using a slide-camera on a tripod, and placed on the platform at such a distance that I could photograph simultaneously the lady launching the ship and the breaking of the bottle. It was always a hectic moment, for if the bottle did not explode the first time on hitting the ship, you had already 'automatically' fired the shutter and had swiftly to change the slide before the lady could grab the bottle and strike again. It took me many launchings before I learnt not to fire the shutter until the bottle actually exploded (with the film camera, of course, it is easy: in a split second you can wind on to the next exposure)—the bottle only breaks once, and you only get just that one chance.

I remember the launching of a naval destroyer from the shipyard of J.S. White & Co on the Medina River at Cowes. Everything was ready, full sunshine, hundreds of people, bands playing, the lovely lady with huge Gainsborough picture hat, her hand delicately poised over the launching lever: 'I name this ship "XYZ". May God bless her and all who sail in her'—pulls lever. Unfortunately the foreman in charge, down below under the platform, had pulled his own lever too early, releasing the ship and she started to glide down the ways, the bottle of champagne still swinging on the platform having missed the bow of the ship by a split second. With the party on the platform staring in horror at the receding ship, the roar of the drag chains, the dust rising in the air, and cheers (and jeers) of two thousand workers watching, all was confusion and panic, and I was left with a slowly swinging bottle on my negative. The drama had yet to be finished. With great presence of mind, one of the directors of the company on the platform released the champagne bottle from its gallows and, taking the lady by the arm, led her gently to the Harbourmaster's launch. Approaching to within striking distance of the huge bow of the destroyer, the lady firmly grasped the bottle by the neck and struck with all her force on the iron box of the ship: the bottle flew out of her hand unbroken and disappeared into the river—all this in full view of two thousand workmen. 'Eh bien, voilà. . . .'

My big camera, meanwhile, had been standing up to the strain of salt air, sea-water and the general banging about that was unavoidable in a small boat. Each winter it was stripped down, rubbed down with wet/dry paper, repainted, metal parts greased, a new rubber ball and tube added, for they perished quickly in salt water. I had thought, of course, about colour photography at sea. There were a few problems. Firstly, the speed of colour film at that time was only ASA8, which was practically impossible to use as it was so slow; also the maximum size of the film was 4" × 3"—'quarter-plate flat film'. However, I was keen to experiment and purchased a folding quarter-plate Zeiss camera with bellows, and a Zeiss Tessar 4.5 lens with six single dark slides. The shutter speed was 1/400th of a second which was enough speed—just—but with an aperture of only 4.5 the exposure was not enough, which meant that I had to incorporate the same idea of using a rubber ball and tube and use 1/250th of a second as shutter speed. This I did, and built a wooden holding-frame around the camera, similar to the one on my big camera. The Zeiss had a wire-frame finder so that I had no need to build a ground-glass finder like the one on the big camera.

I took this camera out on a very quiet day, with full sunshine and the water a flat calm. As luck would have it, a brand new liner, the *Southern Cross* of the Shaw Saville Line, was approaching from the west. Standing on tiptoe, gimballed, I exposed one film only. I rushed back to have the film processed at a colour laboratory. The next day I viewed it—perfect. Of course, it was taken under perfect conditions, but the line company were very pleased with it and we were commissioned to photograph all the fleet of the line and those of other companies operating from Southampton. This was a great help as it enabled me to experiment further financially, and to buy expensive equipment to build a new 'colour camera' especially for the sea.

You may have wondered why we use glass plates as negatives, instead of flat film, film being lighter and unbreakable. We prefer glass plates for various reasons. Firstly, we have found that the resulting negative is harder and has more contrast, which is very necessary in view of soft skies,

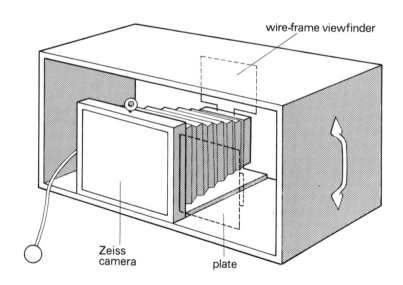

white sails and sometimes light misty days—we need all the contrast we can get. Secondly, in the darkroom glass plates are easier to handle, being firm and not like the pliable flat film. Thirdly, the emulsion on glass is firmer and less liable to scratch in handling and storing. And fourthly, a glass plate does not need to be placed between glass in the enlarger, like flat film, which decreases the possibility of scratching. Finally, it is easier to retouch a glass negative than a flat film.

Another point that I have neglected to make is that we always use one speed in the shutter—the maximum: that speed is around 1/500th of a second, and with the possible variation of light available we adjust the aperture to compensate. This saves a great strain on the brain as there are plenty of other things happening which one has to think about. We don't worry about depth of focus at sea, as most photographs are taken at or near infinity.

The 'Mayflower'

In September 1620, the 180-ton *Mayflower* sailed from Plymouth in Devon, carrying 100 Puritans from England to the New World. After 67 days at sea she reached what is now Plymouth, Massachusetts. Over 300 years later, a keel was laid down at Messrs Upham's boatyard at Dartmouth—the keel of a replica of this *Mayflower* to be built to commemorate the Pilgrim Voyage. It was my commission (and joy) to photograph the launching and sailing of this ship, which was to sail the Atlantic and land the crew on the original Plymouth Rock (some said irreverently that it would have been better if the Rock had landed on the Plymouth Brethren!) On arriving at the building-yard, I found her on the stocks, ready for launching. Comparing her with the lines of the modern yacht which we had seen for so long, she looked positively unsafe. She was built entirely of wood, without a metal fastening in her, the planking being fastened by 'trunnels' (tree nails), 20″ long, made from old cider-casks 130 years old. This age of wood would make sure that there was no shrinkage and therefore no leaking in the hull. All ropes were tarred with Italian Hemp with no splices, throat, round and crown seizings being used only. Sails were made of flax, and all rigging also made of rope only, and tightened by being led through huge 'deadeyes'.

Mayflower

After the bottle of wine was broken open, and the wine drunk from a chalice, she glided down the ways and on reaching the sea heeled over to port at an alarming angle of 30-degree. I think we all thought she was going to capsize, but she just stayed at that angle. The reason was that no ballast had been yet put inside her. Eighty tons of railway lines, cut into pigs of iron, were then laboriously placed in her and she floated trim to her marks. A few days later she sailed on her first trial out of Dartmouth, the sight taking us back many years—337 to be exact.

I must say that Plato's saying—'There are three types of men: the living, the dead, and those that go to sea'—passed through my mind at the thought of her having to cross the Atlantic. However, the crew were carefully chosen volunteers, and I remember that the galley cook was the owner of the famous 'Whig and Pen Club' in Fleet Street.

A photographer was to be carried aboard on the trip over, and I had many interesting talks with him before he sailed. He was a young American commissioned by *Life* magazine of the USA and he was taking with him 300 spools of film (making 6,000 exposures in all). One evening he explained how he thought a camera should be used. 'Keith,' he said, 'I put this matchbox on this table, and I take 100 exposures of it from every possible angle—one of them must be a winner,' 'A strange philosophy,' I said. 'It is like using a machine-gun in the hope that one bullet will find its target. What happens when you have one photo left and the picture of the century appears?'

It shows the difference between an American pressman and a dedicated photographer, and how they think and work. I took exactly six photographs of *Mayflower* sailing and was completely satisfied. She duly sailed across the Atlantic, Captain Villiers at the wheel, with few alarming incidents.

It was a little later in the year that the *Bluenose*, the famous Grand Banks schooner, paid a visit to Cowes. She was the fastest ship of that fine fleet of fishing schooners that operated on the 'Grand Banks' off Canada; they were designed and built to sail fast out to the fishing grounds, fill their holds with their catch, and sail fast back to their home port. *Bluenose* was the pride of the fleet, owned and captained by the famous Captain Angus Walters. She was of 290 tons, 145 feet overall, and had a mainmast of 130 feet. The accommodation below decks was sparse, for storage of fish was their trade. The beauty of the hull-line and proportioned rig were a joy to see and we, with other guests, were invited aboard for a sail around the Isle of Wight. At 08.00 hours we set off eastward, rounding Bembridge Ledge and then on a fine reach to St Catherine's Point. Here we struck a hard south-westerly wind, which put the lee-rail awash. The captain gave me the helm for an hour and I cannot describe my emotions at feeling the heartbeat of that great ship through my hands. The photograph shows her as she was at this time, with the 'dories' stacked on the deck exactly as they were on their fishing expeditions on the Grand Banks. Several of the guests were seasick, and I have a picture in my mind of the 'mate' with each hand gripping the collar of a guest, holding their heads over the lee-rail.

Climbing the mainmast, I was sorry not to have been able to carry my big camera with me, for the view from the crosstrees showed the fine lines

▶

Red Lancer

of her hull to advantage. Rounding the Needles, we broad-reached back to Cowes and, manhandling the mainsail down to the boom, I remember the coarseness of the canvas sails, wet and stiff. It was as if we were endeavouring to fold plywood and I realised why the crew's hands were so tough and horny.

Bluenose finally sailed from Plymouth on her way back to Nova Scotia, but about a thousand miles out she was caught in a violent tempest of 100 mph winds and was hove to for five days, losing everything except her mainmast. With two feet of water over her floors, she managed to return to Plymouth to recover. Many years ago, there was a film called 'Captains Courageous': if it is shown again, I suggest that readers take the opportunity of seeing it, for it is a tale of these Grand Bank schooners racing to their fishing grounds and some of the scenes in very rough sea conditions are superb.

Each year the Island Sailing Club holds a race 'Round the Island', starting in the early morning. Depending on wind and weather, this used to take an average of twelve to fifteen hours, though the time latterly can be considerably less. Four times have I been round, the first when I was a young lad on *Mazurka*, designed by the famous Sibbick. A second time on *Daedalus*, one of the Ratsey fleet yachts which used to sail their canvas out to the yachts in the Solent—I remember being on her bowsprit end and being ducked about six feet under the icy cold water off the Needles. A third time I raced on Dr Crosskey's *Spindrift* with her loose-footed main and gaff-rig. It blew very hard, and many yachts retired with masts going over the side. With our handy rig we went like an arrow, and finished second on handicap to the famous *Evenlode*, sailed by Chris Ratsey. We were annoyed with ourselves for being too exhausted to raise the spinnaker, for had we done so we could have saved our time and been first. The fourth time I sailed on an 8-metre *Armyne*. Off Bembridge, with her deck awash, and myself flat on the deck up to weather by the main rigging, there was suddenly a crack like a pistol-shot and the weather mainstay broke. I quickly looked up at the mast, expecting to see it go over the side, but it whipped like a fishing-rod and stayed like a true piece of spruce, giving us time to come about and effect repairs.

This race has been very popular for years, and 300 to 400 yachts take off each year at the crack of the gun, the variables of winds and tides round the coast ensuring some surprising winners, a case where 'local knowledge' plays its part.

◄

White Gold

I have digressed a little with my enthusiasm for racing, but meanwhile had had some new ideas on my 'colour' camera to be built. Kodak Ltd had by now put on the commercial market a 5″ × 4″ colour flat film—the standard press camera size. This was now rated at a speed of ASA 16, and was therefore twice as fast as the original. Purchasing a Schneider 4.5 lens and shutter-unit at maximum speed of 1/400th of a second, I then built another camera on the lines of my big camera but to the size of 5″ × 4″. This lens-unit was mounted to a circular brass plate which in turn was brazed to a large coarse brass-threaded cylinder to be able to turn and twist for focusing on to the back plate. All parts were designed so that they could be taken apart easily for carrying purposes. The diagram shows the whole concept, and I must admit that it looks at times like a device for conducting a lunar probe.

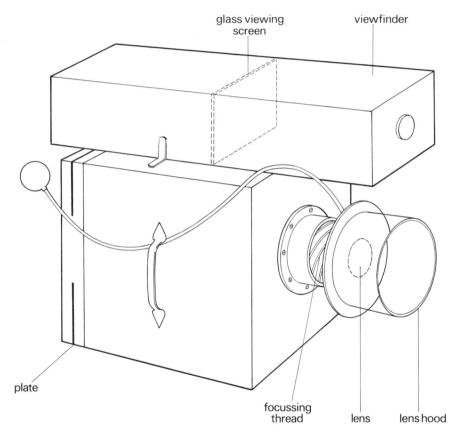

glass viewing screen

viewfinder

plate

focussing thread

lens

lens hood

The camera was an instant success and, as before, the distance-marks were preset, the whole lens-unit being turned on the coarse thread to the requisite mark. We immediately secured a commission to photograph the whole of the Union Castle fleet of liners, which sailed from Southampton to South Africa each Thursday in the late afternoon. The hulls of the liners were of a particular shade of lavender which was extremely difficult to match, due to the sun in the late afternoon giving too warm a colour. Only three months of our English summer were available as the exposure was critical, and if there was a slight haze over the sun no photograph could be taken. Many frustrating hours were spent preparing the launch and camera and slides, and returning with no photographs.

I conceived the idea of flying to Las Palmas in the Canary Isles to photograph these ships as they all called there on their outward passage (their return passage was usually not suitable, as the hulls showed evidence of rust-marks after the return trip to South Africa). Taking a flight by Aquila Airways, a flying-boat service, we dropped down into the bay of Las Palmas. On arriving at the hotel, the first thing to do was to find a totally dark room in which to load all my slides. This is usually a problem, as these hotels are built for the sun and a completely light-tight room is unknown. The manager took me to a building in the garden, with no lighting, and assured me that it was totally dark. Upon shutting the door this appeared to be so, and I proceeded to load my slides. After one hour I happened to look upwards and noticed high up above a tiny circle of light which was not evident at ground level. I hoped this had not reacted on the expensive film. When I had opened the door and accustomed my eyes to the strong sunlight, to my horror I found that the slides were coated with a film of fine dust. I nearly had a heart attack. The building had at one time been a granary. I had no recourse other than to empty all slides, throw away the film, blow the slides clear of dust, and reload them in the lavatory of my room after blacking out all the windows with blankets.

Whilst in Las Palmas I took the opportunity of going to a cockfight—a disgusting exhibition of blood and feathers. I can understand why it is illegal in so many countries. A bullfight was also in progress, the first I had seen. The bulls were tired and emaciated, the matadors hopeless, and the toreadors worse; the only bright spots, according to the cheering crowd, were when the bulls managed to throw the matadors up in the air. The finale came when half the seating of the arena collapsed, causing absolute chaos in the crowd.

I was taking the opportunity of sunbathing one day in the sandy bay when it was invaded by 'Portuguese men o' war', jelly-like sea-objects with a light blue 'sail' and dark blue long tendrils floating at surface level. These tendrils are *very* poisonous, and if they touch your legs they can give you an extremely painful sting. The children on the sands, to my amazement, picked them up by the 'sail', scooped a hole in the sand, covered them over, and then jumped on them, producing a loud popping sound. It is incredible what children do. . . .

A week after I got home, I received a telephone-call at midnight: 'Will you photograph an air crash on the Isle of Wight immediately?' Dressing quickly and picking up a camera and big flash-gun, I drove to the scene of the disaster. To my horror, I found that it was one of the Aquila Airlines flying-boats on which I had flown to Las Palmas a week earlier. 'There, but for the grace of God, go I' was my immediate thought. The aircraft had had engine trouble over the English Channel, had returned by the shortest route to Southampton Water, and had crashed into a hill on the island. The scene was indescribable, with the poor burnt passengers and their belongings scattered over a wide area. I resolved that being a press photographer was not for me.

Of course, if you profess to be a photographer you have to photograph everything. This is exciting and interesting, for you never know what the next assignment will be, and every one is different. I have photographed scars on wives caused by husbands, and scars on husbands caused by wives, hot-water-bottle burns on nether regions for people claiming damages, road accidents, explosions, fires, an infinite variety of subjects. A photographer not only has to produce accurate photographs, but in many instances has to make the subject look better than it really is. Hotel accommodation is a typical example: the lounge has to appear twice as big and twice as attractive, and the best bedroom has to appear as if it was typical of all bedrooms. There was that acutely embarrassing time when the manager showed me the best bedroom at 3 o'clock one afternoon, knocked, opened the door and—er, er . . . found it occupied—Professor Einstein's famous equation passed through my mind: $E=MC^2$ (when two atoms fuse, mass is lost, turning dramatically into energy).

When I got back, I found a telephone message: 'Would you please telephone the Television Centre at Rowbridge, IOW.' This I did, and was asked if I would like to photograph the buildings from the top of the television-mast. Have you ever felt a cold, dead feeling in the pit of your stomach?—well, I replied 'yes' and next day arrived at the Centre.

The mast was supported by four giant cables attached to the mast about halfway up. You had to jump into a box-car which was then wound up one of the cables to a platform. All right so far—but the next half defies you to look down, as you climb up the cold steel-trellis mast, with cameras slung round your neck until you reach a position where your lens will cover the area of the buildings down below. Having strapped yourself on to the ironwork you then look down and see ant-like people on the ground. It's quite exhilarating if you don't mind heights—and I don't seem to. From this height it is possible to see all round the Isle of Wight. However, I was glad to descend, for there is a swaying movement up there, and a stiff whisky in the canteen soon thawed me out.

Our next assignment was to attend the Yachting Olympics in Italy, at Naples. This promised to be interesting. Flying to Zurich, I met an American friend, Bob Shekter, and we drove all day and night, over the St Gotthard Pass, arriving at Pisa at 08.00 hours the next morning. The drive was frantic; the big Italian juggernauts have an unnerving habit of coming close behind you at night, suddenly flashing their headlights full, and sounding off their high-pitched sirens. They put the fear of God into us. We breakfasted at Pisa opposite the leaning tower (my God, and it does lean). Inevitably I took a photo of the tower, for—who knows—it may not be there tomorrow; how long can it stay before it *must* fall? Back into the Volkswagen, the heat intense, shirts and shoes off, driving in bare feet down the autostrada through Rome to Naples.

Bluenose, Grand Banks Schooner, with dories stacked on deck

When we arrived, we found our hotel on the *plage*. The price for five days would have bought a Class I Ocean Racer in England. The first day of the Olympic racing, we went out on the Press boat—never again will I go on a Press boat. With three hours to spare before the start of the racing, we slowly motored out of the harbour. About a mile away, the German Training Ship *Gorch Foch* under full square sails was sailing with the volcano *Vesuvius* gently smoking behind her. Nothing, absolutely nothing, would make that Italian skipper turn and close in on that wonderful sight. We tried bribery, corruption, heroin—we even mentioned the Mafia—but to no avail: we never obtained a photo.

To add to all this, the Press boat was not allowed within half a mile of the Olympic racing, the whole of the world's press was furious, and again—no photos. Now I was becoming desperate. The next day we managed to hire a 'Riva' fast-speed launch at a colossal price and proceeded to photograph the Olympic racing. After an hour an Italian gunboat came to us as if at war, with guns sticking out from all angles. We got the message and, being faster than he was, we were literally chased all over the bay of Naples, finally eluding him by ducking into harbour, tying up the 'Riva', and disappearing into the crowd. And that was the end of the Olympic racing. However, I was content to photograph the competitors before and after the racing, as it was a photograph of each entrant that we really wanted.

Whenever there are any big international events, there are always the perennial thieves and pickpockets about, so I give this word of advice or warning to all photographers: *do not* carry your cameras about in one of those shiny new aluminium cases with 'Nikon', 'Canon', 'Leica', or whatever on the sides. If you have one, paint it black and label it 'Evian', 'Heineken', 'Biscuits'—anything. You won't lose it and the insurance companies will like you.

Again we found ourselves on the autostrada at night, leaving Naples at midnight, and again we met those giant Italian wagons, blasting at us from behind with their klaxons. My American friend had by this time bitten his nails down to the knuckles: in Naples, he always had one eye on Vesuvius which was still smoking gently, and a visit to Pompeii didn't improve his nerves. I asked him later what he thought of Italy, and he replied, 'Jesus, it's got something, but it's a pity it looks so worn'—well, that's a comment about the Old World from the New. My impression of Italy was one full of colour, of richness and poorness (some parts of Naples have to be seen to be believed), but there is a gaiety and way of life in the South that one perhaps misses in our northern countries.

Spindrift

The America's Cup

Much has been written about the 'America's Cup', first raced for in 1851, won by America, and challenged for twenty-two times to no avail. More money and effort has been spent on this cup than any other race at any time. The first challenger that I remember seeing was *Shamrock V* in 1929, when I was 15 years old—I had of course seen photos taken by my father of previous challengers. By 1937 and 1939 we were both photographing the next challengers, *Endeavour I* and *Endeavour II*. I remember *Endeavour II* setting a secret quadrilateral jib a few days before she left for the United States to challenge; by the time she had sailed across, the Americans had copied the sail, and they again won the race.

Now in 1958 there was another challenge, this time by the English 12-metre *Sceptre*. The previous year she had undergone many trials in the Solent. Spinnaker-handling and gybing at top speed was most essential; and to help in this I took some movie-film, strapped down at the very end of the stern and photographing continual gybing. This was then quickly processed and the results shown to the crew the next day. What the crew did not know was that I had photographed their efforts 'slightly slow motion'; and when it was shown on the screen and the times recorded, it made it appear as if their efforts were slow. This was all to the good, for finally they achieved excellent speed.

In the same year we had received a telephone call from a 'M. Herbulot' who wanted some secret photographs taken of a 5½-metre: would we be available? Yes, we would. A week later we went quietly off to the 'Nab Tower' and photographed the 5½-metre with a new and unusual spinnaker. After several trial runs we all returned to Cowes, and it was next

◀

Sceptre, contender for the America's Cup in 1958, trains with her sister yacht, *Evaine*

year that *Sceptre* and *Kurrewa*—another 12-metre—hoisted huge 'Herbulot' spinnakers on their last trials. With these we hoped to win the America's Cup.

It was in this year that I decided to go to America and photograph the Cup races. Preparing for this was almost like going on safari: it was not simply a case of putting your Leica in your pocket and catching the next plane to New York. The 'colour' camera could be dismantled into three pieces, which was no problem—the problem was to carry all the glass-plate negatives, for I knew they were not available in the USA, and weight was the problem. I conceived the idea of wearing a raincoat, to save room and weight in my baggage. I put the coat on my shoulders and filled the two deep pockets—and an inner pocket—with 24 boxes of glass plates. At London Airport I just managed to stagger to the plane, weighing twice as much, it felt, as my normal weight. The flight was uneventful. At the New York Customs, the authorities viewed my camera with a mixture of disbelief, suspicion and derision but I passed through without trouble and took a taxi to my hotel. Now, I had heard about American taxis and their drivers. This one had 100,000 miles registered on the clock, was just one year old and was already a rusty shell of a Chevrolet; and the driver fed me with a continuous half-hour of vulgar stories until I arrived at the hotel.

The next day I travelled from Grand Central Station to Newport, Rhode Island, a long but interesting trip; and I really felt at home when the train rounded a bend and deposited all the coffee-cups, plates, bottles, etc, on the floor. It was just like a heeling yacht, and the fact that I was used to balancing at sea meant that I was the only person left with a *full* glass in my hand.

At Newport, the scene was one of feverish activity for the Cup Challenge. Both 12-metres, *Sceptre* and *Columbia*, were on the slipways having last-minute adjustments made before the first race in two days' time.

Having a spare day, I spent a few hours in the town. Newport is in New England and is more Victorian than England has ever been, both in its houses and in the manner of its townspeople. I remember that it was a hot day and, as I was walking along in a pair of short shorts and a shirt, a middle-aged woman passed me and said, stiffly, 'Haven't you left something off?' This convulsed my American friend, for there is no doubt that the woman was implying that I had forgotten to put my trousers on. The men (and the women) wear those 'Bermudan shorts' which I personally loathe. They always look to me as if they don't know whether to wear long or short trousers and finally decide to cut them just below the knee. Returning to the slipways, I found a crowd of armchair critics around the British yacht *Sceptre*, busily shaking their heads.

Meanwhile, I had important things to do. I managed to obtain a motor-cruiser from which to photograph the first race, but first I had to get authority from the Race Committee to do so. This was easier said than done: once again, the Press of the world were being kept at least half a mile from the racing yachts; having flown from England at my own expense, the Press boat was not for me. I finally managed to see the Commodore of the New York Yacht Club at midnight and stated my case. Stanley Rosenfeld, the American marine photographer, together with his father Morris, had his own boat with special permission to photograph, and I insisted that as there was certain to be a controversial protest (as there always was) during the racing it would only be fair that an English photographer should be able to record it as well as an American. This finally swayed the decision, and now we were ready for the first race.

Better writers than I have described the races, so I shall not attempt to do so. The scene was extraordinary: for four hours before the racing, literally thousands—probably three thousand—motoring yachts were in the vicinity, crossing and recrossing the course before being shepherded half a mile outside a circle around the triangular course. This resulted in the sea in the area of the racing being absolutely confused: the wind was light and a permanent criss-cross of waves from every direction combined with the hot atmosphere from all the exhausts of the yachts, to give an unreal atmosphere to the scene at the first 'gun' of the first race.

The jockeying for position at the starting-gun is always contentious in the America's Cup Races, for being in the weather position at the start allows one to keep the other boat pinned down, and one tacks all the time with the other boat to keep just on his weather bow. I regret to say that *Sceptre* was nobbled in each race, and *Columbia* pointed a little higher to weather, making the end result certain to be a win for America. Between races, *Sceptre's* mast was shifted to try and improve her performance, but to no avail; and that was one more challenge lost. I obtained my photographs of the two boats together at the start of each race, and then separately under the spinnaker and on the wind, allowing me to complete the history of photographs of every challenger and defender since the inception of the race.

One interesting fast launch which was used for ferrying the crews to the yachts caught my eye—an 8-metre open launch with a 'deep V' section, which was riding the waves so comfortably at any speed that I photographed it from many angles for future use. It was, so I learned later, the first launch of a 'deep V' section to be designed by that famous American designer Ray Hunt. More about this later.

Before leaving Long Island Sound, I took the opportunity of visiting 'Marblehead' and met the famous American yacht-designer Hereshoff in his house overlooking the bay. It was fine to see his house, on the walls of which so many of my father's photographs of most of Hereshoff's beautiful yachts were in evidence and we had many hours' discussion on the performance of these great yachts.

I returned to New York by car and spent my last evening with friends who plied me with various drinks and deposited me, bloated with food, in the aircraft at literally the last possible minute. I only woke up as we passed over Cork, in Ireland, where the aircraft began its final descent to London Airport. Sitting next to me by chance was obviously, by his brogue, an Irishman, and I asked him if it was true that the *poteen* (that red-hot whisky distilled illicitly in the woods of Ireland) was ever allowed time to mature. He replied: 'Sure, and b'Jesus they sometimes let it get cold.'

What do I remember about America? Well, the hotel lift which took me up to the twenty-fifth floor at such a speed that I thought my feet would go through the floor. Then I recall the occasion when I wanted to cross the street without using a pedestrian crossing (something that one does so often in London) and narrowly missed being shot by a policeman's Colt .45 for having infringed the traffic regulations.

When I got back to my Solent stamping-ground, it was to get back in harness. The firm of Saunders-Roe, who had built so many aircraft for the two World Wars, had produced the 'Lerwick' flying-boat and a very fast and manoeuvrable 'flying-boat jet'—a single-seater flying-boat for use in foreign waters. These were very difficult to photograph for, as before, one never knew just when the aircraft was about to take off from the water, and the photographs required were always to be taken just as she lifted clear. We had some really frustrating days in the launch, with its maximum speed of only eight knots. To cap this, the firm then built the great 'Princess' flying-boat—the biggest flying-boat in the world. This huge aircraft when launched looked like something out of the classic books of HG Wells. On her *first* taxiing trials in the Solent, the test pilot, after taxiing for half a mile, suddenly opened the throttles, and in three minutes she took off, without any effort, astounding the hundreds of onlookers. When I spoke to the pilot later, he told me that he just knew that she would fly so he let her go. . . .

I, meanwhile, had been becoming more and more frustrated with the speed (or lack of it) of my launch; having had an air-sea rescue launch capable of 30 knots during the war years, I knew the value of speed. My mind was also on that launch that I had seen in America, designed by Ray Hunt: one day I was talking to Bruce Campbell at his yard in Hamble about this launch, and he said, to my surprise, that he had the concession to build this exact launch and was in fact doing so. Messrs Fairey Marine were mass producing the cold moulded hulls, and Bruce was completing the final launches and calling them 'Christinas'. Now Bruce Campbell has done so much for powerboating, and if he accepted a design like this then he knew exactly what he was doing; so I ordered a hull from Messrs Fairey

Marine and had Bruce Campbell to complete it. No double bed in the cabin and no grand pianos; just one luxury: a lavatory. The launch was to be powered by a 100 hp Perkins Diesel engine. I had no desire for a petrol engine, apart from the cost of fuel; and there should be no chance of fire aboard as normally I like to photograph by myself and have a free mind.

On trials, the *Christina* logged 25 knots maximum, with a cruising economical speed of 18 knots. She was dry in rough weather, stable and, with the diesel, reliable—in fact, just what was wanted. Like all boats, these launches have their little problems: the cavitation of their propellor necessitated having a new one every season; and the propellor being unprotected, we hit our usual number of underwater objects including empty champagne bottles. All yachtsmen, please note: if you must throw bottles overboard, fill them with water so that they sink to the bottom, out of harm's way. One day you might hit your own.

The type of hull on the launch became the forerunner of the powerboats that were to follow. It was 23 feet long, fairly full forward, and tapered to a deep V-section aft. Four 'runners' from bow to stern, two each side, were glued and screwed on the underwater hull, allowing the hull to rise quickly at speed and break the surface tension of the water to the hull. The beam was eight feet, and the cockpit, which was at knee-height, gave plenty of room to operate. The cockpit was self-draining through two scuppers in the transom above water level. There was a single control for ahead, neutral and reverse. The cabins of these launches were big enough to take a large triangular bed—as Bruce said, 'large enough to have two people to sleep with you'. . . . A lavatory, wash-basin, minimum cooking facilities and a hanging locker for oilskins completed the equipment.

The propellor-shaft was a straight drive through to a P-bracket and cutlass-bearing. The diesel engine was water-cooled, similar to a car engine, the exhaust system being cooled as normal by a sea-water inlet. All spare ropes, fenders and boathooks I always fix securely. I cannot over-stress the importance of this, as I once stepped on a rolling boathook and tore the ligaments in my ankle, which kept me ashore for six weeks.

Powerboat Racing

The *Christina* opened up a greater area of coverage for photographing, and I could now operate in the English Channel and outside the Solent in general. It also opened up the photographing of powerboat-racing, which had just started. The International Power Boat race from Cowes to Torquay and back is now an annual classic. The first race in 1961 was won by T.E.B. Sopwith in *Thunderbolt*, virtually a larger *Christina* (30 feet), designed by Ray Hunt with a 650 hp engine. I was still using my big black box of a camera, and with the 'ball and tube release' it allowed us to obtain critically sharp photos, with my launch travelling at 20 knots and the other launch doing perhaps 50 knots. You have to remember that we operate under the same conditions as the powerboats and often lift off the water exactly as they do, which allows no second chance of getting another photo.

Surfury, 1965

Let me describe, from the photographer's point of view, the typical powerboat race of the early 1960s. There might be as many as fifty powerboats taking part, and our object is to photograph each one if possible, catching them jumping off the top of a wave, showing a clean pair of propellors (for this is the action shot they like). Studying the course the night before, with the weather forecast, direction of wind, state of sea, angle of sun, etc, you have to determine where to be to catch them at their best. Having worked it all out the night before, the morning dawns, the forecast has changed, and you have to plot your best position all over again. We decide on the Needles Channel at the west of the Isle of Wight; there is most likely to be rough sea there, as the channel is narrow and all the powerboats are more or less on a straight course. We set off at 09.00

hours, the start at ten o'clock, giving us an hour to get ahead of them. The sun will be behind them which is not good, but there will be action where we are.

In the distance can be seen three helicopters, with the daily Press aboard, hovering over the leaders. In minutes it seems that the boats are upon us, each one leaping and swerving, crashing and leaping again. With camera ready, one hand on the wheel and one on the accelerator, we have to jump into position—that exact position to show them jumping clear of the water, exposing their rudders and props. We become as bruised as they by the time we have finished, and it's all over in minutes, for the leaders are bunched together, all going at 60-70 mph and water flying everywhere. Have you ever tried shooting even one flying pheasant with a .22 rifle? It is comparable—you hardly ever get one. If you do, you deserve a gold medal.

A point that must be appreciated is the danger of being in the path of these high-speed powerboats. Latterly, speeds of 70-90 mph have been attained; and as the boats jump from side to side off an awkward wave you cannot expect them to keep a straight course, and so you must keep your distance. One incident involved the powerboat *Jackie S*, driven by four marine Jaguar engines, which ran completely over a spectator launch, incredibly without loss of life to the occupants. Their comment is worth putting on record: 'We must be the only persons to have been run over by four jaguars at the same time and have lived to tell the tale.' This *Jackie S* was destined for trouble, for the next year I had her nicely placed in my viewfinder, off the Needles, when she swiftly turned to ninety degrees port and headed for the Needles Rock at 50 mph with 1,000 gallons of high-octane fuel aboard. Her rudders had jammed, and she stopped a few feet from the Rock, just as a man was seen to lower a large fender from the lighthouse on the Rock—whether to save the boat or the lighthouse I never knew. . . .

The sudden enthusiasm for powerboat racing was interesting. Engine-power had always been the limiting factor before. Now boats had to be more or less flat-bottomed to attain any speed, and this on relatively calm water. As soon as the water became a little rough, boats broke up, their flat hulls being unable to stand the punishment. Suddenly, it seemed, engines were being built with much greater horsepower, which necessitated radical changes in the design and structure of the boats themselves. Ray Hunt of America, as previously mentioned, developed the 'deep-V section', which was called 'The million-dollar-bubble ride': this gave a great cushioning effect and quite revolutionised hull design for fast speeds. It may not be appreciated by readers that a flat-sectioned hull travelling at say, 30 knots, when hitting even small waves, feels as if it is hitting solid objects—water is at times as hard as concrete. If the boat jumps six feet in

the air and lands slightly on its side, the crew, necessarily standing freely, come down with the boat at various angles, and the punishment is great both for boat and crew.

With the modern powerboat, with its much faster speed, it is even more punishing for the crew: the continual pounding compresses one's vertebrae; and ribs—occasionally even legs and arms—are broken. To help combat this heavy and damaging punishment, leather-covered foam padding one foot thick is packed round the cockpit, hydraulic cushioning floors are fitted to take the shock, and crash helmets are worn, by order, for

◀

Filming powerboat racing (*Photo:* Bob Searles)

Dry Martini, perhaps the most famous of the Class 1 power boats

if you hit the water at 70 mph it is as if you are hitting a brick wall. At this sort of speed these boats traverse the surface like a ricochetting bullet—the impact on re-entry can be as much as 7g or 8g: enough to break knees and ankles.

My memories of photographing in this field are fascinating. When you have worked on ultra-secret hulls, with their multiple reinforcing members, their moulded fibreglass sections, the fitting of the engines, the propulsion-units and steering mechanisms, you almost become an expert in the art yourself after photographing them year after year. Our great powerboat helmsmen 'Tommy' Sopwith, 'Sonny' Levi, Don Shead, for example, and Americans Jim Wynne and Dick Bertram, Italians Carlo Bonomi and Sig. Balistinieri, most of them designers in their own right, all have that special item called courage. For to drive these powerboats (even in some of the sea conditions that we have been out in) at anything between 60 and 90 mph produces tremendous physical and mental strain.

Carrying 1,000 gallons of petrol, driven by up to four engines, in a thin wooden shell on rough seas at high speeds, I asked one of the racing drivers his opinion of this kind of racing. His answer: 'It's the second best thrill in the world!'

Danger? Yes, plenty of it. I remember Sir Max Aitken power-racing off Miami and going through a wave which swept down the deck, smashing the windscreen and sweeping the crash helmets off the three crew in the cockpit. They were fortunate not to have lost their heads as well. I also remember Don Shead and Vic Miller, his engineer, in their powerboat *Delta* racing off the shores of Miami. She had a tail-fin rather like that of an aircraft, held in position by two wire stays, port and starboard. Flying above them at the start of the Miami Nassau Race, I saw the port stay break: the tail-fin held for a moment, broke off at the base, and then started to thresh about in great sweeping slashes like a giant cut-throat razor on the end of the wire stay, nearly decapitating Vic Miller in the cockpit.

It was also Don Shead and his crew who had to jump for their lives when one of the driving shafts of their powerboat *Thunderfish* fractured and drove itself through a fuel tank. The powerboat immediately caught fire with the possibility of a huge explosion. She burnt down to water-level and then sank as a total loss off the south of the Isle of Wight.

Jim Wynne, the well-liked American designer and driver, ran into trouble when he was leading the race to Torquay. His forward water ballast tank refused to fill. Having nothing to keep it trim and level, his boat *Ghost Rider* started to plunge and leap out of the water. It was during one of these plunges that his mechanic Robert Sherbert smashed both his ankles. However, Robert insisted that Jim drive his boat at maximum speed to victory for another eighty miles—a story of courage and extreme agony.

The week before this epic race to Torquay and back, the area of water between Hamble and Cowes is alive with these 'hot rods' shooting and screaming across the water, testing and blowing valves. Con rods pass through crank cases, and engines are removed with feverish regularity and replaced with spares. The Italian team bring a large wagon full of mechanics and spares—a virtual travelling workshop. At Fairey Marine Yard, Hamble, all one can see is 'bottoms and legs' protruding from engine-hatches. At Souter's Yard on the River Medina the story is the same, with last-minute adjustments being made throughout the night—it must resemble the pits at Le Mans. The Solent hums with the noise of distant high-pitched exhausts, and the scream of the over-revved propellors as they jump out of the water is only matched by the screams of the pure sailing fraternity as yet another delicately-held spinnaker collapses to the wash of another 'hot rod' passing. It is noteworthy that in about 1850 the Royal Yacht Squadron was reputed to have made a rule that 'any member owning a Steam Yacht should automatically disqualify himself from membership' and later, when steam yachts were allowed, a rule that 'if over 100 tons, all steam yachts should consume their own smoke'. I've no doubt that some people today would like to make a rule that 'all powerboats should consume themselves'.

However, all things come to an end, the day of the race dawns, the forecast is rough, and the crews look a little thoughtful with knowledge of a rough ride ahead. The start is again a classic: it is a rolling start from a point half a mile away from the actual start-line. *Brave Borderer*, the Naval turbine gunboat, as a marker at the end of the line, cruises at fifteen knots and increases slowly to fifty knots as she hits the line and then peels off; and the line of power-boats is away for that punishing race of nearly 250 miles. With the increasing speeds of these powerboats, and the condition of the seas on which we had to operate, we had to accept that our launch and technique could not compete. We realised that the only answer was to photograph from the air. I know of nothing so fascinating as sitting outside a helicopter, with one's feet on the landing pontoons, a seat belt around the waist, a few feet above a Class I powerboat, watching it leaping at 70 mph into the rough seas off Portland Bill. Having experienced these seas at 25 mph in my launch, I know exactly the feeling: you actually wince as they slam down into the next wave, you 'feel' the crack of the crew's ribs against the side of the cockpit, their knees buckling, stretching, and buckling again on the next slam down—and all this for a racing distance of 236 miles. From the helicopter, it is as if you were in an armchair. On the end of a skyhook you can position yourself (if you have a good pilot) at 15 feet in the air and follow along, taking photographs from all angles of the boats leaping into the air. The only trouble is expense—at £2.00 per minute flying-time it is not peanuts, but you get exactly the photographs you want. In case you have been given an impression of egoism in this book, don't be deceived: it is not egoism but pure unadulterated enthusiasm and dedication mixed with a little masochism and egoism that enables us to think we've obtained our objectives—the action, excitement and sparkle of colour in photographing these powerboats is its own reward.

When photographing the building of yachts, commercial craft, and so on, I had the opportunity of meeting some of the real craftsmen of England, especially in the building of lifeboats, and to see the variety of woods that were used. When visiting the yards of the Royal National Lifeboat Institution at East Cowes, I had noticed on the bank of the river cut trees and branches, trimmed but lying about in glorious confusion and in a variety of shapes. Nearly all were oak, and I was told that they were valued very highly for it was from these, when cut at the sawmills, that all the sweeps, curves and knees were made that are so necessary in the building of fine boats. Today there is a great change, for two reasons: firstly, the lack of original material, the oak; and secondly, laminated pieces of section are so easily made and glued with today's strong glues, giving cheaper and stronger construction. Very often the whole keel from stem to stern consists of one laminated piece, with all its curves and thicknesses.

Hulls, especially of racing yachts, where the planking was originally of oak or teak or mahogany, are very often now being built by the cold-moulded method, consisting of cross laminations screwed and glued around the original frame. This gives great strength with lightness—a typical example was *Surfury* which was built in this manner, its light but strong hull being able to combat travelling at 70 mph in rough weather, slamming into the seas of the English Channel.

It is absorbing to photograph and portray the craftsmanship of these vessels while they are built, for each boat is different and generally one has to employ a different technique to show the fine detail of workmanship and the increasing use of glass fibre in the strengthening of the hull. I love the feel of wood, but regrettably, the oaks, teaks, spruces and variety of mahoganies are slowly disappearing in hull form, giving away their soft touch to that of hard, bruising fibreglass.

In a yard in Miami, a few years ago, I visited a factory that was producing powerboats made completely of fibreglass. They were being fabricated by workmen who might well have been making washbasins on an assembly-line; I don't think there was a sea-going man among them—a depressing sight.

However, let us not despair, one has only to look at some of the latest beautiful yachts from the drawing-boards of Nicholson or Sparkman and Stevens to see that all is not lost, for they are fibreglass built. It is fascinating and almost unbelievable to know that the great production yachts of Sparkman and Stevens, made in Europe, are being built of fibreglass in the heart of a forest in Finland; the trees must be writhing in exasperation—or joy.

On the eastern side of the mouth of the River Medina at Cowes there has always been, as long as I can remember, the active firm of S.E. Saunders, later Saunders Roe, builders of fine aircraft and boats. Over a lifetime I have seen many mysterious things emerge from its large hangar-like doors, the first being the 'Bat Boat', the first amphibious flying-machine designed by Sopwith, made up (it seemed) from pieces of wire and string; but in effect it was a single-seater flying-boat. Colonel Seagraves' famous powercraft *Miss Britain*, which broke the world speed record, next emerged, followed by a series of 'Saro' seaplanes and finally by the 'Princess' flying-boat mentioned earlier in the book. Now mysterious 'goings on' were happening behind closed doors; there were strange noises and stories in Cowes, and talk of an infernal machine was rife.

Finally the doors were opened and revealed 'the Hovercraft', as a journalist wrote in a daily newspaper, 'looking like the Graf Zeppelin upside down, with the nacelle on the top and dirigible underneath'. Many months of the deafening noise of aircraft engines then started, followed by letters to the Press, demonstrations and manifestations, but all to no avail. When a project is sponsored and financed by the Government it must go on. Businessmen in Cowes could not carry on a telephone conversation, so they shut their doors and retired to the local pub to drown the noise in drink until the infernal machine went to sea.

Many experimental machines were built at the start of this project, and I remember one pilot succeeding in turning one over whilst on test. Those dining at the Gloster Hotel that evening found the hotel rising to the occasion; on the menu was 'Lobster a la Hovercraft'—a cold lobster, served on its back on a bed of lettuce.

However, these were early days and we now have small machines running regular passenger services in various coastal resorts; and there are also the big monsters carrying passengers and cars across channel from Dover to France and back without mishap. The motion one experiences when aboard is peculiar and difficult to describe. Another journalist wrote that it was like 'riding on a pregnant woman'—a not inaccurate description? The small craft still do not have complete control when they have a Force 5 wind up their tail. I remember one coming into Cowes from Southampton, missing the hoverport completely. It was last seen disappearing crabwise up the river at a high speed, and it probably ended up in Cherbourg. I think there is no question that the actual idea of the hovercraft has a future; and I have recently seen a comment that the Navy are experimenting with the possibility of using one as a fighting machine,

probably travelling at over 100 mph. Interesting. . . .

Another winter's work passed, spring came, with its rain showers and cloud shadows flitting across the white wavetops. The weekends of racing were starting to increase, building up to another Cowes Week in August. Saturday, Sunday, two wet, nasty days with a south-westerly gale—no photos. Monday, still, quiet and a fine misty rain—no pictures. Tuesday, Hallelujah! a bright north-westerly day with a promise of the wind backing to the west. My son Kenneth and I prepared for some action today: full sun, a Force 4 from the north-west, and giant cumulus clouds as a perfect backdrop—this was what we wanted. The Class One, Two and Three Ocean Racers sliced their way through the short seas down to the west, the sun now in the south spotlighting and highlighting their wet decks— action all the way, short whipping tacks with cries of 'Water', 'Starboard', and 'Lee Ho' being cast by the wind. At West Lepe buoy, on a fast ebb, all was confusion, and yet not confusion as they rounded the buoy and stemmed the fast west-going tide. 'Spinnaker up, genoa down and then up tallboy' came the cries from the helmsmen—now for some wonderful action. The wind had meanwhile increased to Force 5.

A fine German yawl with mizzen, mizzen staysail, main, spinnaker and staysails set starts to roll, first to one side and then to the other, main boom end in the water, then 'spi boom' end on the starboard side in the water, on and on for a mile. The crew are on their toes—a little tense, perhaps— waiting for the inevitable: it happened. With the spinnaker boom end dipping deeply below the surface, there was a splintering crash and the boom flew into matchsticks. Another Class I racer, with her spinnaker flying high, overpressed with too much canvas aloft, starts her long roll from side to side—with no boom vang, the mainboom rides up and up, the wind catches it to leeward and it slams over in a fantastic gybe. 'Christ! If somebody had been standing on the deck, he would have been decapitated.'

In the distance we see *Rendez-vous*, a flicker of red dipping and lifting in the distance. Approaching her, we see she is taking some terrific 'knock downs', rising and draining the water through her scuppers. The excitement is electric, the sheets are squeezing the water out under their enormous tension, something's got to go. She takes another knock down, broaches and shoots round 180 degrees through the eye of the wind and charges us with all sails aback—we who have been shooting her through her lee quarter, beat a hasty retreat. That day was like a day's game-shooting, the 'birds' rising under one's feet and skittering off at all angles, each a rare and stimulating sight, an absolute ballet—of the sea.

Rendez-vous, 1971

The Tall Ships

'And then one day I had a job to do
Down below bridge, by where the docks begin,
And there I saw a clipper towing through,
Up from the sea that morning, entering in.
Raked to the nines she was, lofty and thin,
Her ensign ruffling red, her bunts in pile,
Beauty and strength together—wonder, style.'

John Masefield

'Tall Ships'—what impressions are conjured up in one's mind on seeing those words? The Greeks were supposed to have said that 'the two most beautiful things in the world are women and wine'—if only they had seen a full-rigged ship, with thousands of square feet of canvas urging her through the water, they would have added that to their list. I have always admired paintings and etchings and the occasional blurred photograph of the early windjammers, *Pamir, Passat, Archibald Russell*, the great grain ships which sailed the oceans of the world in their majestic urgency. Returning to the Isle of Wight one afternoon, by ferry, I saw in the distance a great four-masted ship anchored off to the east. On reaching the shore I immediately jumped into my launch to go and see this wonderful sight. Approaching her, I made out the name *Pamir* in great letters on her bow. I immediately asked permission to come aboard and the German captain gave me a friendly wave in welcome. I'll try and give my first impressions—a newly-honed and scrubbed deck, seemingly half a mile long; four huge masts of steel towering into the sky with an absolute mass of rigging, rope, wire, yards and furled sails. Each of her four masts at the

Pamir

133

base took three men fingertip to fingertip to encircle it. On the yards were young lads, seemingly seventeen or eighteen years old, with their feet on the bolt ropes high up in the sky, 120 feet off the deck, calmly furling sails as if they were rolling cigarettes in the wardroom below. It recalled a verse of 'The Dauber' by John Masefield—

> A hundred and fifty feet above the deck,
> And there, while the ship rolls, boldly to sit
> Upon a footrope moving, jerk and check
> While half a dozen seamen work on it;
> Held by one hand, straining, by strength and wit
> To toss a gasket's coil around the yard,
> How could he compass that when blowing hard?
>
> And if he failed in any least degree,
> Or faltered for an instant, or showed slack,
> He might go drown himself within the sea,
> And add a bubble to the clipper's track.

There was such an air of peace and contentment aboard ship—no smell of diesel, just fresh air and quietness, broken only by the sighing of the wind through the mass of rigging, and the smell of tarred Italian hemp. I was in another world of a hundred years ago.

I asked the captain when he was sailing and if it was possible to arrange a time for a photograph with full sail (I felt as if I was asking the Queen for the Crown Jewels), but he said that he would most certainly let me know—they were anxious to sail and were waiting for a navigator to fly in from Germany. Two days later he telephoned me to say he was leaving at midnight and therefore there would be no opportunity to photograph— and now that picture will never be taken, for on her return trip from the Argentine she was caught in an unpredicted hurricane and lost with practically all hands. Nearly 300 lives were lost, one or two cadets being the only survivors from this terrible tragedy. Our photograph of her at anchor is probably the last taken of her.

Captain Alan Villiers, that great mariner who served most of his life 'before the mast', speaks in his book *Voyaging with the Wind* of the great sailing ships: 'She is gone from a heedless world for ever—not so much discarded with all her challenging skills, but allowed to quietly disappear and the loss not even noticed'—not so, Captain! It has been more than noticed, and perhaps it is this that started the formation of the 'Sail Training Association', with the intention of rallying these great ships and crews of all nations together every two years in a different port.

The first rally of the Tall Ships was scheduled to be at Dartmouth, and the thought of seeing a number of these fine ships, all together under sail, began to foment in my mind, two or three days before the event. Having driven down, I arrived on the quay at Dartmouth and was immediately transported to another world. *The Sagres, Christian Radich, Flying Clipper, Amerigo Vespucci* and the Danish *George Stage,* with many others, were lying quietly in the River Dart, within a stone's throw of the quay. The scene was indescribable—sailors from all nations in their varied nautical uniforms, their officers in long scarlet cloaks over their uniforms, a dozen different languages being spoken, longboats being rowed to and from the quay and the whole scene set against a backcloth of the Tall Ships. Here was a chance to record this for future generations, for these ships will never be replaced.

Two days later, on the morning of the race, the ships set sail from Dartmouth to rendezvous off Berry Head. Now, I have learnt—the hard way—that it pays to photograph as soon as possible, for it is no use waiting for a horse at the last fence if he has broken his leg at the first, and the ships were clear of all the thousands of spectator launches awaiting them at the start, so I secured some photographs of them immediately. The start was of course classic: bright sun, enough wind to push them majestically at six to seven knots. This gave me time to change my slides, still using my big camera, to obtain photographs of them miles out to sea with every sail set from top-gallants to studsails. These ships naturally presented an entirely new image to me, and it was only by remembering some of the old classical paintings that I had some idea of the best angle from which to photograph.

The next race of the ships was two years later, starting at Brest in north-west France. I decided to go there and complete my files on one or two ships that I had been unable to obtain at Dartmouth. Travelling by train from Cherbourg to Brest (a thing I shall never do again), we stopped at every possible 'halt', envying more and more the local French eating their 'sandwich jambon' and drinking their 'vin ordinaire', becoming hungrier and thirstier each hour as there were no restaurant facilities on the train. However, arriving at Brest, there were the Tall Ships alongside the quays, an absolute hive of activity. Having hired a small fishing launch for the next day, I returned to the hotel and found my old friend Jack Frost, that inimitable marine correspondent so beloved by everybody, complete with straw boater hat. It was later in the evening, walking through the town of Brest, we were amused at what was obviously a baby shop, called *Pre-Natale,* and on the windows of which, carefully written in large letters, were the words EVERYTHING FOR THE BRIDE. Well, they organise things differently in France, evidently. It reminded me of the printed notice that I had seen in the office of the director of the Electricity Corporation in Cowes, just after the war. There was of course a shortage of civilian personnel during the war, and the Electricity Corporation had sent out a notice, which the director had had framed on the wall. It read: EVERY ADVANTAGE SHOULD BE TAKEN OF YOUR SECRETARY IN THE LUNCH-HOUR.

Tall ships gathering

I digress—Jack Frost and I had arranged to go out together the next day, he to report on the ships' race and I to photograph. Morning dawned, and we went to our fishing launch. I think they must have been fishing that night because the boat was covered in the remains of a haul of sardines. Realising that the speed of the launch was a maximum of five knots, we went to sea two hours beforehand to be nicely in position for the Tall Ships when they started. Looking astern, we could just see the ships starting to be towed out. The weather was perfect, strong wind and sun, and we were very enthusiastic at the sight we were about to see. As the ships drew level with us and gradually passed us we were waiting for them to haul up sail, but the minutes passed and passed, and they were merely being towed further and further out into the open sea. We suddenly realised, that with the slow speed of our launch, we were not going to get a photograph at all, and eventually they disappeared out of sight into the English Channel. There was only one thing to do after that: turn back and head for Brest, and open the case of wine. By the time we reached harbour, full of wine and covered in sardine remains, the two impeccably-dressed Englishmen that had stepped aboard were unrecognisable. Jack Frost, to his credit, wrote a glowing article on the start of the race, how beautiful the ships looked, especially the *Amerigo Vespucci* with every sail set, etc, etc. I thought he wrote very well, not having seen a thing—which shows the advantage of being a journalist instead of a photographer.

Stopping our return journey in Brittany for a day, we tasted the delights of this north-west corner of France. The little ports and bays are a delight for any camera-conscious person, the people are charming, and of course the food and wine are excellent. Now, we know that the Italians kiss anything that moves. In this part of France, the French eat anything that moves—larks, thrush, squirrel, frogs, snails, snakes—and their *pâté de grive,* if you happen to find a good one, is delicious. They tell me it is made from one thrush and one donkey—in those proportions; it is still delicious. On the other hand, if you had seen, as we did in a restaurant, the lady opposite (admittedly of Teutonic appearance and proportions) bite, with a hollow echoing crunch, through the skull of the bird encased in the pate, and then delicately remove the beak from her mouth with her fingers—as we say in England, 'it makes you think'.

The sea-food, of course, is legendary in Brittany. Crab and lobster, langouste and langoustine, are plentiful, brought fresh from the sea, cooked, and put on your plate, with a glass of *blanc de blancs*—that is the ultimate. It was in Brittany that I had my first oyster. Now, in common with many people, the sight of an oyster used to deter me from ever eating one. It was Alain Gliksman, the well-known French helmsman, who, after two bottles of wine, persuaded me to sample an oyster—and I have not stopped since. They taste like mud, of course, but very good mud.

Two years later, there was to be a big rally of the square-rigged ships ending in Kiel, Germany, to coincide with the Olympic Races. When we arrived at Kiel, the day was perfect, the wind blowing straight into the harbour, which meant fortunately that the ships would have a dead run into Kiel. Bright sun completed the scene, and way out in the distance one could make out on the horizon what appeared to be either square blocks of white flats or the Spanish Armada, depending on one's imagination. Within an hour these white shapes materialised into the ships—nearly twenty of them in line astern under full sail: fully-rigged ships, barques, barquentines, schooners, every type of rig imaginable, the most majestic sight ever to have been seen, these ships from fifteen different nations. One travels all over the world to find these ships and then suddenly, in one day, they are all presented to you on a single plate.

Back at Cowes, cruising in the Solent one day, I saw a small square-rigged ship, a Russian, furl her sails and dropped anchor off Cowes. Coming alongside her to make my 'number', I noticed about thirty Russian sailors aboard, under the direction of a hard-featured woman who was heard to say, pointing at the same time to Cowes, 'That is where all the English Lords and Ladies live'. . . . Needless to say, the crew were not allowed ashore—incredible!

It was later in the week, still looking for subjects to photograph, that I noticed a very attractive-looking motor-yacht approaching at a speed of about twenty knots. With our usual green flag flying from the stern, identifying that we were 'Beken—Photos', I gently eased my launch across to her. As I approached nearer I noticed that she started to slow down. This was annoying, for she looked superb, and as I closed in even nearer she suddenly stopped. I came close to him and indicated that I wanted him to speed up to enable me to take his photo: To my surprise he said, 'Oh, sorry, I thought you were a wreck-marking vessel with that green flag'—how one's ego can be deflated in a second!

A Change of Camera

It was about 1969 that we were seriously thinking of a change of camera. The 'big box' had done its job and was gradually becoming unable to compete with the much faster sailing and power craft that we were being asked to photograph. The fast catamarans and powerboats were too rapid for us to cope with changing the slides of the camera quickly; it needed a less cumbersome and therefore necessarily a smaller camera to cope with this problem. A smaller camera of course meant producing a smaller negative. Our type of photography had always been regarded as a type of portraiture at sea; as in a studio, the large negative facilitates easier retouching and sharp enlargements. Original glass negatives were 10″ × 8″ in size, and there were no enlargers as we know them in the early days, prints being made by contact. It was only when the 'projection printer' was invented (now called an enlarger) that smaller cameras came into use.

I do not know of any other branch of photography that has to operate under such adverse conditions as ours. Forget the gentle sunny days, when a good record can be obtained by most photographers, but take the other days of which there is a high percentage: the seas can be cold and wet (especially in winter); the sky is cloudy with patches of sun; the boat approaches in sun and as you lift your camera the sun disappears; you adjust your lens aperture and again lift your camera—the sun comes out again; again you adjust your lens aperture; spray flies up from the bow; you duck your camera and wipe the spot of water off the lens; your sailing yacht has passed you; you accelerate to catch up with it; and as you lift your camera she comes about on the other tack, and you repeat the whole process over again. Besides all this, you are watching for a good bow wave

Kruzenshtern, on her way from Plymouth to New York, Operation Sail, 1976

139

on the yacht, making sure that no sail luffs are shaking, no ropes hanging over the side, and wait for that shaft of sunlight to strike her (which makes all the difference between a photograph and a picture)—and all this has to happen at that one second when you take your photo!

We were commissioned to take photographs of all the new lifeboats built in the area, and the Lifeboat Association also required colour slides to be taken for their records. For this we were using a Leica 35mm camera. As I have said before, miniature cameras are prone to letting in salt water, and they don't like it. Inevitably on some occasions the camera, in rough weather, had more than its share of salt water—of course you wipe it quickly, but you can't wipe the water that has infiltrated through to the mechanism of the shutter and diaphragm, you just offer up a prayer. On principle, we always fix an ultra-violet filter over all our lenses as a protection against damage, for it is much cheaper to replace a filter than a lens.

Well, we had to make a decision: what camera were we to use for a smaller format? The best proportion of film for yachts is 6″ × 9″ used upright and horizontally; most of the cameras available were just not practical for continual use at sea, which was one of the reasons that we had designed and built our own. The most practical ought to be one that takes the standard '120' film both in black-and-white and colour, if only for the fact that supplies are always available in any country and at reasonable cost.

Handling most of the cameras available, we came to the decison that the Hasselbad, although 6″ × 6″ in format, must be the most practical. The removable back, which enables one to change rapidly from black-and-white to colour, was an important factor, and the camera itself is as near mechanically perfect as possible. It is also heavy, which is good from our point of view, on sea and in high winds. It is a single-lens reflex camera which allows you to see through the lens the subject that is being taken, and the camera is robust. It doesn't like salt water thrown at it, of course, it is expensive, and it's a square format; but if they can send one to the moon to take the photographs that it did, who am I to complain?

Now, any camera is only as good or bad as the person who uses it. The 5″ × 4″ colour camera with the rubber ball and tube was, and still is, being used; but of course with the Hasselbad camera one reverts immediately to the 'eye-level' type of viewfinder. I have said before that one usually ends up with one's subject at an angle of 45 degrees on the negative using this type of viewfinder. However, with years of handling cameras at sea, we found that we had attained a natural gimbal action, succeeding in keeping our horizons absolutely level. When you are always on the sea, you develop a technique of keeping the salt spray out of the boat and therefore out of your camera: waterproof containers, plastic bags, grease on the

▶
The start of a power boat race

140

camera—all were discarded as being cumbersome. You have to use your camera very quickly at times, and even grease to protect the metal parts is not good for it eventually finds its way on to the lens and film—and of course the camera is also likely to slip out of your hands into the sea. The technique is to learn how to handle your launch so that virtually no spray comes over you. You should use the launch as you use the camera—it becomes part of you, like a third leg; it moves with you and you advance and retire quickly in any direction. This means that the efficiency of your launch and engine is the guarantee of your income, sometimes your life, so it must be kept in impeccable condition. To give you an instance, for photographing a 'Marseilles Week' I had hired a launch from a local boatyard, and inevitably it was late in being put into the sea for me. There were no ropes, no fenders, no anchor, no signalling flares—nothing aboard. I had just five minutes before the start of the race to buy a length of terylene rope before proceeding to sea. The Mistral was blowing directly into the harbour at about Force 6, bright sun, perfect for action photography. After one hour at sea, in extremely rough conditions, the engine stopped and would not restart. For an hour I tried to start the engine; the launch meanwhile was being blown quickly towards the rocks at the entrance to Marseilles. Fortunately a big power catamaran saw me in difficulties and by good sea-handling caught my rope and towed me from the danger of being impaled on those rocks, which would have meant loss of boat, camera and a sticky time for myself. On examining the engine, a Volvo Z-Drive, I found that the petrol contained about twenty-five per cent fresh water in the tank, which had been filled by the boatyard!

Insurance is absolutely necessary for 'Third Party', which reminds me of an accident I observed, about which I cannot give too strong a warning. On sunny days at the weekends many people take to the sea in fast runabout launches with outboard engines, with a child (or adult) sitting on the bow with their legs hanging over the water. At a minimum of 25 mph it feels fine, with the sea and wind rushing by UNTIL the engine suddenly falters or hits an underwater object, the boat suddenly drops speed, and the child goes over the bow—then nothing can stop the propellor running over the child's body underneath. The accident I saw resulted in the bad mutilation of both feet of a child who had been sitting on the bow of just such a speedboat, and the 'damages' were enormous.

Mention of sunny days recalls an invitation that I received to go to Antigua in the West Indies and photograph the 'Sailing Week' which operated from 'English Harbour', the famous port of call for Lord Nelson. English Harbour is one of the great homes of yacht chartering, and it is these yachts that were to be photographed for brochures and general publicity. An old Chinese proverb says 'A journey of 1,000 miles starts with but a single step', and with that one step I was transported 3,000

miles to the Caribbean. I made contact with the pilot of the Super Trident
VC10 when we were approaching Antigua and had a view of the islands
which people rarely see—from the cockpit of a huge airliner. I remember
the pilot flicking a tiny switch, the size of a peanut on the instrument panel,
and the huge aircraft banked 45 degrees, as if being steered by the hand of
a giant. Landing and disembarking at Antigua was like walking into a
sauna. The heat was intense after the coolness of England. On my way
through customs the coloured officer looked at my camera, wiped a wet
finger across the Hasselbad lens twice, for what reason I do not know; but
if I had had a gun, there would have been an unfortunate 'death at the
airport'.

The Nicholson family met me at the airport—the kindly family who
have done so much for English Harbour and the charter business in
Antigua—and in half an hour I was immediately catapulted into a 'rock
session', accompanied by a steel band until four o'clock in the morning.
My first impression of English Harbour is therefore somewhat hazy as the
local rum was exceedingly good and the company excellent. However, on
waking up the next morning, I climbed above decks (having been berthed
overnight in one of the charter yachts) and saw one of the most wonderful
sights—dozens of beautiful large sailing yachts, moored stern onto the
quay of the harbour, the whole harbour being surrounded by palm trees.
These yachts had slowly disappeared from England and the Mediterranean years before, and here they all were, as new, bright paintwork, new
varnished teak, all back to their original condition.

It is said that everybody to do with the sea passes through Antigua at
some time—and I can well believe it. Everybody should go to the Caribbean before they leave this world. English Harbour was the harbour to
which Nelson took his ships for refitting. It is a tiny harbour, invisible from
the sea a quarter of a mile away, and it is said that when Nelson's ships
were inside small palm-trees were fixed to the tops of the masts to give the
impression of palm-trees when viewed from the sea, camouflaging the
ships within. The original 'dockyard', with its slipways and big capstans,
storehouses and ammunition-houses, is still in first-class condition. The
ammunition-houses were interesting, being solidly built of stone, with
semi-circular roofs, three feet thick, to protect them from the shells of an
enemy.

The next day the whole of the charter fleet set sail, the weather perfect in
the Caribbean setting, and, sailing in line, we photographed each yacht
under perfect conditions. Darkness seems to fall at the drop of a hat in the
West Indies, so the evenings were given to less serious things, such as
dancing and swimming and drinking in the 'Admiral's Inn' to the strains
of the local steel band, with, in the background, the eternal hum of the
insects.

Having a free day next morning, all the charter yachts sailed up the coast to a small island and moored off the sandy beach in a perfect lagoon. Our skipper, Andy, had caught a big fish on the spinner of his fishing-line on the way to the island. He then rowed ashore and gutted the fish at the water's edge and prepared it ready for the evening barbecue. Everybody was swimming and sunbathing in this delightful bay, when we heard a terrifying piercing shriek from one of the girls who was seen frantically swimming for the shore; a baby shark, about a metre long, could be seen in the shallow water, and it had made a grab for her leg—she had the teeth-marks to prove it. This cooled us down very quickly and we stayed out of the water for the rest of the day, realising that it must have been the smell of the fish-guts that Andy had thrown into the water that had drawn the shark to the bay. As we made our way back in the early evening, two large dorsal fins could be seen on our port side about ten metres away—a chilling sight.

These yachts sail down south through the islands as far as Grenada, and in this most southerly island are found most of the spices of the world— an island that I think everybody imagines in their dreams, and one which most yachtsmen cruising across the Atlantic make their first stop from Europe.

Regrettably, these things have to come to an end—and back to the cold winter of England, from 35 degrees to 10 degrees. The trip leaves one unsettled, for the life in the West Indies seems so perfect. However, it was time to haul my own launch out of the water, put her under cover and work on her, stripping and painting, ready for launching at Easter.

In England and Northern France, due to the cool and moist winters, racing usually begins about Easter and finishes in October; insurance is less costly when the boat is on the land and not subject to the continual wear and tear of the sea. Of course more and more marinas are being built and more yachts are staying afloat all the year under safe conditions, but this does not stop the ice and frost and general salt air from attacking the wire and steel rigging. The increasing number of fibreglass hulls now being built do not absorb water as much as the conventional wooden hull.

Now it has been said that a yachtsman is a person who stands on the stern of his vessel, in a marina, tearing up £20 notes—IN THE RAIN. But I think this could apply to most dedicated sportsmen, whether sailing or skiing. Marinas are said to be expensive. They are, of course, compared with what yachtsmen had to pay before; but the convenience of stepping aboard or ashore directly from the boat, with all the gear and without the inconvenience of having to use a dinghy and outboard, and also the fact of a safe anchorage twenty-four hours a day with no worries for the boat's safety when one is a hundred miles away—all this compensates for the

cost. Ideas had been forming in my mind, with two other 'compatriots' of Cowes, of the possibility of a marina being built in Cowes, to take the place of the mooring piles which had been in existence for some years. In Cowes Week, when there is an influx of more than 500 yachts, these yachts were sometimes moored 20-abreast between piles fore and aft. When a strong wind blew from the north or north-east, the chaos was indescribable, as present and past harbourmasters will confirm. Bowsprits broke, covering-boards split, ropes snapped, yachts broke away and beat each other to pieces. It took many years of investigation, tests, drilling and planning for the original ideas to come to fruition; now, less than a decade after being built, we wonder how ever Cowes existed before, and this is true of so many marinas.

I can speak from experience, for it was in one of these sudden vicious north-easterly gales that my *Christina* sank at its moorings one October morning; I was powerless to do anything about it, the seas being too rough to launch a dinghy to get aboard. I had the heartbreak of watching her go down; it felt as though I had lost an arm. She was recovered two days later by local divers, with no actual damage done, but of course the engine had to be stripped down as a result.

I have also neglected to mention an incident of fire aboard one evening: halfway across the Solent, the engine suddenly started to falter. Looking astern, I saw a lot of black smoke coming from the exhaust. Immediately I cut the engine and opened the engine-hatch, to find a small fire burning in the engine-tray in the bilges. Fortunately we carried a small pocket fire-extinguisher in the cabin: this gradually extinguished the fire, allowing the engine to cool. I could not think how the fire had started—no petrol, no electrics, nothing to start the fire. I started the engine again, and after a minute examination of all parts of the engine, suddenly noticed a very fine pin jet of oil from an armoured flexible pipe in the lubricating system shooting directly on to the hot iron exhaust exit-pipe. I came to the conclusion that this hot oil had been vapourising on the hot exhaust pipe, and that my opening the hatch cover had admitted oxygen from the air, immediately causing the flash-point and consequent ignition of the oil. Patching the tiny jet with a piece of aluminium foil and Scotch tape enabled me to reach home.

Three points emerge from that exercise; firstly, there is always a chance of fire in a boat, even with a diesel engine; secondly, always carry a fire extinguisher aboard, however small; and thirdly, the engine should be immediately accessible—you should not have to unscrew flooring or covers to get to it. Also, having seen a new diesel-engined 38-foot motor yacht burn down to the keel recently, the crew having to jump overboard to save themselves from fire, life-jackets are a necessity. It wasn't a pretty sight. Fire at sea is frightening, for one just cannot walk away from it as on land.

Alain Colas and Keith Beken on board *Club Méditeranée*

A New Launch

When you have photographed so many different types of craft, you carry in your mind the type of launch that you are ultimately looking for. In my mind it should first of all be a good sea boat, the type of boat to go out in any weather; it should be safe—by that I mean unsinkable; it should be as dry as possible and also fast; and it should offer good all-round visibility. Looking in the Italian yachting magazine *Nautica*, I noticed a photograph and a description of a launch which looked as if it was exactly what I wanted. The Genoa Boat Show was taking place the following week and I took this opportunity of flying to Genoa to examine this launch.

It was the newly-designed 21-foot 'Boston Whaler', with a fine entry bow section not at all like the well-known Boston Whaler. . . . The hull was very stable, and the steering and driving console was positioned one-third of the length of the boat from the stern (the nearer he is to the stern in a powerboat, the more comfortable it is for the driver); one or two outboard motors could be fitted to the transom according to speed desired; she was unsinkable, the floor of the launch remaining well above sea level at all times, and she had a large self-draining exit at the stern in case of taking a large sea on board.

Samphire, 1973

Inevitably I ordered the boat to be sent to England immediately, and she has proved to be one of the finest sea-going launches, fast (30 knots) and safe, riding any sea in gale-force conditions. Recently, off Marseilles, with the Mistral blowing Force 7, she rode the high and rough seas perfectly at any angle to the wave conditions, enabling me to obtain with little effort, by myself, all the photographs I desired.

It is probably as good a time as any to mention my thoughts on this business of marine photography. You are of course self-employed, which is an enjoyable position to be in. (Or is it, with recent governments?) Naturally you rise or fall entirely by your own efforts; there is no 'state aid'. It is an extremely personal job to do—rather like an artist, for he cannot employ another person to paint his pictures for him. Many more hours are spent in the darkroom than on the sea, in case the reader imagines the life is all at sea. Additionally, my being also a chemist ashore causes a little difficulty; but, as one British Member of Parliament once said, 'If you can't ride two horses at once, you are no good in this bloody circus.'

One is entirely dependent upon the weather: on fine sunny days everything is relatively easy, but it can be completely frustrating (as happens many times) when one has an appointment to photograph a large beautiful yacht, with only that one day available for various reasons, and the weather turns out to be rain or fog, or no sun, or no wind. You can always take a photograph, but it is only a record and not a picture, and the photographs do not enhance your reputation. Unfortunately the sea is not like a studio, where extra lighting can be added, a test photo taken, and the camera mounted on a tripod with various spotlights around.

It must be evident to readers that in photographing big racing events, and with the increasing international competition, 'incidents' and anger could be caused if the photographer were not aware of the potential dangers. The photographer MUST be in the game, knowing every move that is going to be taken (or *may* be taken) by the craft surrounding him. Secondly, the photographs have to be taken as the crew-members would like them—no collapsed spinnakers, no sail luffs shaking, no fenders or spinnaker bags hanging over the side, no forestays sagging down to leeward, no spinnakers in the water as they are being gathered in, no racing flags at half-mast—how the hell do you get a good photograph? You might well ask. The answer is that you wait and wait and finally you get your picture. If you don't wait and take care of all these points, the crew, on seeing the photographs, say 'Yes, it's a pity about that spinnaker, etc', and you don't sell your picture. Racing crews and owners are very proud of their racing craft, and they have every right to have top-quality photographs taken of them—by any photographer. One does not accept a photograph of one's debutante daughter displaying a hole in her stocking, so the marine photographer has to 'delicately' make signs to the yacht telling him that he has a fender hanging over the side, or some other fault that would spoil the photo. I remember once asking a past Commodore of the Royal Ocean Racing Club if he would mind hoisting his mainsail up another foot (I felt as if I was chiding the Pope on the quality of his communion wine).

With the use of a smaller camera, it is now possible not to change but to

Uffa Fox tries out the new Fox Canoe, 1936

add to the variety of photography at sea. It allows one to move in close and show the action on deck: the crews 'sweating in', the 'coffee-grinders', the foredeck hands 'snaffling' the spinnaker down on deck as they round the next mark close.

If you look at yachting photographs over a number of years, and if you have raced yourself, the photographs are interesting to examine, for you can see in an instant why certain yachts are winning yachts and others losers. The losers can be seen, for example, to have the 'spi pole' too high in the air, or sails tacked down loosely, or sheets hanging over the side, or the 'spi' still hoisted when it would have been better to have set the genoa (an old racing skipper once told me that it was like running a 100-metre race and tying up one's shoelace at the same time). All too often you see crew-members just sitting—at no time is there nothing to do on a racing yacht.

It is essential that you should know when the racing yachts are going to be at their best for photographing, and this for the very reason that you cannot afford the time or the expense of photographing the yacht two or three times and then on the next leg of the race see her two miles away with spinnaker, mizzen staysail, 'tall boy', smoking along with her deck under, looking the picture of the century. Here it is necessary for the photographer to have taken part in the sport so that he knows exactly when the yacht *will* look its best in relation to the sea, sun and wind. You also have to learn to contain your frustration, when, having exposed your last roll of film, the bloody wind rises, the bloody sun shines, every yacht hoists it's bloody spinnaker, and every bloody crew is shouting to have its photo taken. You can't win. . . .

Meanwhile, 'back on the farm', two sons had suddenly started to grow moustaches, which meant that they were growing up fast. The elder took to underwater diving, passed various courses and technical instruction, and finally found himself qualified as a deep-sea diver, diving off Norway and then finally off Peru. The second son, having fallen into the sea at the age of six, absorbed enough sea water never to have got it out of his system; so he was sent off to a photographic college to learn the basics of photography, and in a very short time was back and is now deep in the marine photographic business with me.

Now, I have always preferred, for various reasons, to be alone when photographing. Many sea-going people, more seasoned than myself, have commented on this unfavourably, but, as many will know, when you are by yourself your thoughts and actions are concentrated entirely on your objective to the exclusion of everything else: the boat and yourself become one person; you move and drive your boat as you would use a third arm. If you accelerate or decelerate violently you have no crew to worry about and, most important, your ears and eyes are concentrating exclusively on the other boats cross-tacking in close proximity. Also, perhaps most important of all, the photographer wants to be in just that one square foot of water to shoot his photo, and nowhere else, and most often there is no second chance. This solitude can only be bettered by having someone who thinks and acts exactly as oneself—and who better than one's own son?

On a lighter note, we often spend hours at sea waiting for a client to arrive by appointment. I always carry a mackerel fishing-line aboard, with eight feathered hooks of varied hue. One day, waiting off the Needles for a late appointment, I threw the line over in Scratchells Bay, just south of the lighthouse. The weight had not even touched bottom before they struck— those of you who know will understand the electric shock that shoots up your arm to your brain with the speed of light when eight mackerel 'king-size' hit the hooks at the same time: you just can't pull that line in fast enough for they all jump in different directions. Within thirty seconds of dropping that line, I had mackerel, blood, fishscales and cameras all in glorious confusion in the cockpit of the launch.

Cowes Week came and passed; new exciting yachts, both sail and power, were making their appearance each year. One morning there appeared an impressive piece of machinery riding at anchor, a huge Russian hydrofoil straight from the Volga, carrying a hundred passengers. It was stange to see, in our 'capitalist' waters, the Red Flag flying within a stone's throw of the Royal Ensign of HMY *Britannia*. The officers on board were more human than on the square-rigged ship: they welcomed visitors, giving trips at sea running high on the hydrofoils. In the evenings there was no shortage of whisky and vodka aboard—in fact they were short of water, something which did more for *detente* than any of our politicians have ever managed to achieve.

While on the subject of guests being entertained aboard ships at cocktail parties, etc, I should mention that the Royal Navy have a fine tradition of putting the gin into the water jug, and the water into the gin bottle, so that, having given you a small portion of 'gin', they then give you a large amount of 'water' from the water jug. The idea, of course, is to start the party swinging early—and it does. I remember one time . . . well, actually I cannot. . . .

'No Cure for Sea~Fever'

This book could not be complete without a chapter on Uffa Fox. Having lived within gin-and-tonic distance of him for most of my life, and he now in a better world, I want to pass on his love of life and adventure and his irrepressible humour to those young people who follow.

When I first knew Uffa, he was in charge of the 'Cowes Sea Scouts'. They could not have had a better teacher. The Sea Scouts had been given, with Uffa's help, an original whaling longboat, the *Valhalla*, 30 feet overall. The boat had been rowed many thousands of sea miles in the recovery of whales. Uffa's first escapade was to take nine sea scouts sailing across the English Channel and up the River Seine to Rouen, thus giving the lads a good grounding in seamanship and general boat-handling. Over a period of many years they then cruised the south coast from Dover to Land's End.

At the age of twenty-three he and four others took the 35-foot *Typhoon* across the Atlantic, at one time having a near-180° capsize in a storm. Uffa was washed overboard, and saved himself by clinging to the mast and sliding down it to the deck as she came upright.

He was apprenticed to the fine shipbuilding firm of S.E. Saunders at East Cowes, and it was from here that he accumulated many ideas for his later boat building, during the construction of the high-speed *Maple Leaf* and the record-breaking *Miss Britain II*, driven by Colonel Seagrave.

Living on an old ferry-bridge on the River Medina, Uffa started to rebuild racing dinghies of laminated mahogany, using oiled silk between the laminates for waterproofing. He then designed a racing canoe of the same materials to challenge for the Canoe Championships of America. Building two, he and Roger de Quincey then took them to the United

Uffa Fox

States in 1935 and swept the board after some brilliant racing.

A few years later, he built a double-sliding-seated racing canoe, and, with Bill Waight as crew, sailed her across the Channel, complete with cooking stove and stores, to the Brittany Coast, from Cherbourg through Granville, St-Malo, Portrieux, Ile de Brehat and thence to the Ile de Bas—300 miles through calm and storm. As Uffa said, 'I know nothing more enchanting than flying low over the water on the end of a canoe's sliding seat at 12-15 knots.'

I have already mentioned his breakthrough in design in building the first dinghy ever to plane on the surface, and he continued for many years to build the winners of the 'Prince of Wales' trophy for 14-foot dinghies. To test these cup winners, Uffa would wait for a Force 5-6 to blow in the Solent; he would then telephone me and say 'See you outside in half an hour, Keith'. Donning his oilskins, he would launch his dinghy and plane down the Solent with me taking photographs from my launch, both of us finishing like a couple of drowned rats.

His boatyard at this time was at the end of Birmingham Road, a few doors away from me, and directly opposite the Police Station—I mention this because there were many 'exchanges' with the Police Force which are legendary and far too numerous to recount, his character being 'extrovert' to say the least. His 'stretching' of the law resulted in occasional appearances at the Police Court where, after a fine from a benevolent judge, he always made a donation of £25 to the Police Benevolent Fund in court.

Uffa was irrepressible. Opposite his boatyard, in the road, was a circular stairway disappearing into the ground, leading to a 'Gents WC', but having no visible outward sign to that effect. It was Uffa's invariable sense of humour that led him to indicate to all foreign clients that they should take the 'Underground' *(Metro)* to Southampton on leaving, by that stairway.

During the war years, as already mentioned, it was his active and dynamic drive which led to the building and immediate acceptance by the Air Ministry of the airborne lifeboats. Uffa would never approach the 'bottom rung of the ladder', but by sheer enthusiasm apply at the top; and it was this that enabled the lifeboats to be completed so quickly for air rescue.

In later years, Uffa became the sailing companion of HRH the Duke of Edinburgh, racing his Dragon *Bluebottle*. He also initiated the young Prince Charles into the delights of sailing. Then he designed his 'Flying Fifteen' class which gave a new impetus to small-keel boat racing. Coweslip, raced by the Duke of Edinburgh and crewed by Uffa, became a familiar sight at Cowes Week, and I recall at the 'Review of the Fleet' one year many elderly nautical eyebrows being raised by the captains of the warships at the sight of a tiny sailing yacht being sailed through the middle of the Review by Uffa, the eyebrows only being lowered as the tiny yacht luffed up and came alongside *Britannia*.

Uffa will remain known through his designs (as will many other designers) but it will be the man that will be remembered: his outlook on life, his language—never bad but earthy—his great sense of humour, and above all his love of people and the countryside. Amongst all the books that he has written, his *Joys of Life* and *More Joys of Living* are a tonic. His love of animals, particularly his horse 'Frantic' and his retriever 'Bruce', reminds me of his riding to hounds in the Isle of Wight, and the sheer fun that he derived from it. It also reminds me vividly of the occasion when an elegant American lady visiting Britain was very anxious to meet this remarkable man of whom she had heard so much. She was told that if she happened to be in the 'Buddle Inn' at Niton on Friday morning at one o'clock, there might be a chance of meeting Uffa. The day arrived, with the elegant lady sipping a Martini at the bar of this very nice old inn. At one o'clock the door burst open and in rode Uffa, with his shock of hair and dressed in hunting pink, on his horse 'Frantic'. Dismounting, he ordered a pint of beer for himself and two for his horse. At this moment his retriever 'Bruce' came bounding in and, true to form, placed his very cold and wet nose straight between the elegant lady's skirts. . . . The chaos was indescribable.

Uffa's house on the edge of the Solent was always 'open house' to anybody and everybody, and so, walking into his lounge unannounced as I was expected to do, one never knew who one would meet. One day it might be the Admiral of the Fleet, the next some old friend who had seen better days, being wined and dined, and the next the late young King Faisal who was so cruelly assassinated and with whom we had had a happy time photographing, sailing with Uffa. The grand piano was always covered with sheet music and plans of sailing yachts in glorious confusion, and the fine old pieces of furniture showed his love of finely-designed and carved wood—and yet I remember one remark of his: 'The material things of life are not essential, and money becomes a necessary evil; in this world it seems that the less things we need and have, the happier we are, for then everything but the bare necessities are luxuries.'

I remember the BBC wishing to do a filmed interview of Uffa sailing his Flying Fifteen. With all the cameras and crewmen on my launch we went out into the Solent, Uffa sailing his craft ahead and connected by a long thin microphone-wire to the recording-machine on my boat. You will realise the difficulty of trying to keep an exact distance behind him as he planed ahead of me. The laughs were loud and long at the remarks being made by Uffa to his crew and to me, all of which were recorded and most of which had to be erased. I suspect that somewhere in the files of the BBC that original recording remains; it was too good to erase.

    In the last years of his life, we looked through many racing photographs together, and his observations on the racing tactics, or lack of them, as shown by the photos were more than accurate. One day he said to me, 'Keith, in my life, I've now met everybody and done everything, and now I'm satisfied.' That was not the remark of an egoist, but a man who had led a full and active life in doing just the things he wanted to do. In his 70th year, still climbing into his Flying Fifteen for a spin on the Solent, I asked him what it was that kept him so active. His answer? 'Keith, there's no cure for sea-fever.'

▶
Scaramouche

Romantica

Big Apple

Trans-Ocean Racing

Races around Britain, races to the Azores and single-handed races across the Atlantic had started to raise their heads. In 1960 the first single-handed transatlantic race from Plymouth to America had taken place, a distance of 3,000 miles. It took place every four years and became increasingly popular. The size of the yacht was only governed by the condition that it must have sailed a distance of 500 miles solo. In 1972 *Toucan*, a tiny ten metre sloop, was sailed across by Alain Gliksman, competing against a great giant of a three-masted schooner, *Vendredi Treize*, 39 metres long, designed by Dick Carter. Flying in a helicopter above the *Vendredi Treize* produced an extraordinary impression of this modern racing machine with no person on deck (the single occupant, Yves Terlain, was probably having his *pastis* below).

In 1976 an entry had been received for an even bigger four-masted schooner, 245 tons and 72 metres long (nearly twice as long as a 'J' class) named *Club Méditerranée*, which was to be sailed by Alain Colas. She was designed by Marseilles architect J. Bigoin and built at Toulon. I went to see and photograph this remarkable vessel; she was built in three sections, upside down, on the slipway, and then welded together. When finished, she resembled something out of the film *Jaws*. I must pay tribute to the designer and the dockyard at Toulon, for when she was launched she slid gracefully into the water with no problems—I think the first time ever that a yacht of this size has been launched upside down.

To photograph this great hull I used a 'wide-wide' angle lens. Fortunately there was a giant travelling crane above the hull, and you reached this by climbing up a cylindrical ladder 75 cm in diameter—which left

Pen Duick at Cowes Regatta, 1974

163

little room for greatcoat and cameras carried on the shoulder. One hundred and three steps later, I vowed again to give up cigarette smoking; but the view was good, and you could really see the lines of the yacht from this height. Alain Colas was enthusiastically hopping about on crutches (he had sustained a bad accident a few months earlier aboard his own yacht, his anchor-chain whipping around his right ankle, all but tearing it from his leg. Sometimes these things happen even to such a highly-experienced seaman as Alain, who had just been round the world single-handed without mishap. His courage and enthusiasm must have been sorely tested, for he had only a few months left before the 500-mile trials in which to get back to top form). The hull was then towed into the yacht basin where, by the simple expedient of wires round the hull and from the tip of the keel, she was gently turned to a vertical position and then rolled with a tremendous splash into her normal floating position with deck uppermost.

If you look at the results of the single-handed transatlantic races—

1960	40 days, 11 hours	Sir Francis Chichester (GB):	
		Gipsy Moth III	39 feet
1964	27 days, 3hours	Eric Tabarly (France):	
		Pen Duick III	45 feet
1968	25 days, 20 hours	Geoffrey Williams (GB):	
		Sir Thomas Lipton	56 feet
1972	21 days, 13 hours	Alain Colas (France):	
		Pen Duick IV	70 feet
			(trimaran)
1976		Eric Tabarly (France):	
		Pen Duick VI	75 feet

—you notice that each year the winning boat is larger and the winning time faster.

Whilst on the Mediterranean coast, I took the opportunity of driving along the Cote d'Azur, taking the prettier coast road. My first 'welcome' was a newly-painted white wall on which an 'artist' had sprayed the words *merde au tourisme;* being somewhat of a Francophile and having experienced the traffic, I almost appreciated the comment. Arriving at the well-known (certainly by name) St Tropez, I found this attractive harbour packed with the most glamorous yachts—also nude and semi-nude bodies, most of which don't seem to go swimming, but whose silhouettes are good. Prices in the restaurants seemed high of course, but I was told that if you look carefully at your bill you can find the waitress's telephone-number included. . . .

Photographing at sea in the Mediterranean is somewhat frustrating. Winds are normally light, and the very high sun throws deep shadows on the decks of the yachts (except in early morning or late afternoon). The results are inclined to be 'hard' or 'contrasty', so different from the soft skies and clouds of England. The big yachts in Cannes, Nice and further along the coast in attractive Villefranche and Monte Carlo, produced a feeling of nostalgia, for all the big yachts had originally been based in England, perhaps thirty to fifty years ago. Seeing them berthed at the quays here reminded me of all the fine photographs that had been taken of them in their heyday: *Creole, Sayonara, Xarifa*—they are all there, and although they are in excellent condition I have the feeling that more gin flows on their decks than sea-water.

The Admiral's Cup

1975 was another Admiral's Cup year. This series of five races was started in 1957 and is organised by the Royal Ocean Racing Club. It takes place at Cowes every other year, its aim being to encourage international racing. Each country can enter a maximum of three boats. The five races are divided into three inshore and two offshore, the last of which is 'the Fastnet' (for which triple points are awarded). In 1975 twenty countries were represented by sixty of the finest racing machines, each one the last word in design, from nations as far apart as Brazil, Argentina, Australia and the USA. It was our aim (and delight) to obtain action photographs of these boats in particular, in addition to the other 500-odd yachts racing during the Week.

The competition for the Admiral's Cup is not just keen, it's red hot. It was said that in 1826 the town of Cowes held a race for a gold cup. During the race two yachts from different countries fouled each other, causing the crews to set about each other with marlin-spikes. The spirit of rivalry in the Admiral's Cup is just as intense, but I think that one day it will not be so much a matter of marlin-spikes as of a straight, clean bullet.

To operate among this fleet of highly competitive racers you need to be part of them, to think as they do, to be able to anticipate their tactics seconds *before* they carry them out. If not, the wrath of God will descend upon your head when you get in their way, not to mention having an international incident on your hands. Those who have seen the start of the 'Fastnet', with its sudden unleashed fury at the crack of the starting-gun, will have seen these sixty racing machines, locked in mortal combat, tacking and cross-tacking each other with just inches to spare down the

◀

Blizzard

167

rocky shore to the west, while the winchmen are sweating their guts out to get that last inch in on the genoa. And here we are in the midst of it all—like being in the path of a herd of wild deer, their lean heads plunging 'nostril under the sea'.

And now here comes the latest challenger from Brazil, and there is another just astern of us, her stem bursting through a wave, jetting spray either side—the crack American ace *Salty Goose* with her sister *Charisma* just under her lee. We keep half an eye on the German *Saudade* coming at us to port, and the other half on the Frers-designed Argentine *Wa Wa Too*, just coming about to starboard. Ahead is *Maverick*, about a boat's length away with deck awash, the crew snuggled down on the weather deck, waiting for the next 'Lee Ho!'. *Ginko*, the Australian favourite, shoots across our stern; a shout of 'Watch it, Beken!' drifts to our ears—it was close enough but they know us by now. And so it goes on down the Needles Channel, the boats slowly separating, clearing their wind each from the other, the crews settling down for those long hauls ahead, way down to Land's End and round the Fastnet Rock perhaps sixty hours later. Hulls, sails and rigging are now so similar in design that it must be the helmsmen and crews who will decide the winning boats. We slowly surf back to Cowes. This has been the last race of the Week, an eventful week of calm spells, occasional rain and good, stiff breezes; we are content.

Ashore, after each day's racing, there are the continual cocktail parties, dinner parties and what-have-you. The 'Squadron Ball' goes on into the early hours of the morning, its 'castle' and elegant lawns softly lit for the event. Taking a last gentle stroll past its entrance just after midnight, I was the lone observer of an American sailor, rolling up the steps of the landing-quay (as only an American sailor can roll); slightly inebriated, he crossed the fine lawn to the lofty oak-tree in the centre, and, gently swaying, urinated against this hallowed British oak. If the tree could have spoken about this desecration it would not have confined itself to 'Yanks, go home'—but instead it stood, swayed slightly, and recovered in true British tradition.

It is impossible to describe or capture with a camera the atmosphere of Cowes Week: the sounds of the brass cannon at the foot of the 'Squadron', the wind through the 500 yachts moored close with their forest of silver and gold spars reaching high, the scenes ashore in the evenings, the remarks of the contestants catching the ear—such as that of the American trying desperately to get more ice for his Scotch: 'Goddamit, you Limeys have been afraid of ice since the Titanic'. Then there are the liquefactious conversations in the cockpits of the racing craft: a comment from *Yeoman's* crew—'The last time we were on the Fastnet it blew so hard we had tea on the mainsail'; from Tiger Nye of the *Carina*—'Coming over from the States, our spinnaker was set so perfect for five days that when we downed it we found a seagull nesting on the top.' And there are other interesting remarks, such as when the crew of the *New America*, that lovely schooner built to the lines of the original, claimed that on the way over from the USA they had logged fifteen knots non-stop for four days—which could well be true, if you think of the clean wake she leaves when travelling at speed. And amongst all those modern racing machines you will see stealing into harbour, unheralded and anonymous in the dusk, with red and green glinting on the dark water, a tiny three-ton sailing cruiser, not very glamorous to look at, its engine pop-popping—but, no matter how small or ugly, it is somebody's boat, bought with money carefully saved, to let its owner sleep his nights aboard or just to be—on the sea.

Five days later we are off to Plymouth to see the first-comers arriving from the Fastnet. It is always a fascinating sight to see the finest ocean racers in the world congregating in one area after nearly a week of a hard and competitive race. Crews examine their photographs, commenting on their competitors' bad crewing.

Let us look for a moment at the list of Admiral's Cup trophy-winners over the years:

1957	Britain	1969	U.S.A.
1959	Britain	1971	Britain
1961	USA	1973	Germany
1963	Britain	1975	Britain
1965	Britain	1977	Britain
1967	Australia	1979	Australia

These results are interesting, for the Fastnet usually decides who is to win the Cup. In this race, local conditions are of no advantage to anyone— you can choose any designer and/or builder for your yacht, the only necessity being that the crew of the yacht should be nationals of the challenging country. It would seem at the moment as though Britain has the edge on the other countries.

Meticulous attention to detail is necessary when photographing these racing craft. No sailmaker wants a publicity photograph showing his sails as ill-fitting or stretched. Makers of winches want *their* winches shown on the winning yachts. The makers of paint want the gloss on the hull to be of the highest quality, and of course the boat designers themselves want photos showing their boats to advantage, at their best and not lying on their ears in a gentle breeze. Ah, well. . . .

It was now time to return to the Mediterranean, to photograph the racing at 'Marseilles Week' and then on to the sailing trials of *Club Méditerranée* at Toulon. April weather, two glorious days of sun and wind, and 150 photographs taken with the new Hasselbad. . . . When I came to

Club Méditeranée

process them the next day I found to my horror that all the films were blank: the great 'Rolls Royce' of cameras had failed and all the time and effort had been in vain. On examination of the lens/shutter unit, I found that the shutter spring had broken. The camera contains two shutters, one between the lenses and the other in the body of the camera: this latter shutter makes a loud 'clap' as it operates, masking the sound of the shutter which had broken (it's an automatic reaction to listen to the noise of the shutter being fired when photographing). I suppose you can't win everything in this world; I can only be thankful that the Hasselbad put down on the moon did not fail. Fortunately the shutter could be repaired quickly, and the sun and gentle breezes increased for the rest of the week.

I bless the day that sailmakers started to introduce colour into their sailcloth—especially on occasions like the day I saw, approaching from the south, *Phantom,* born and raised in Miami but racing under Italian owners. With every stitch of sail that she could carry, she sailed majestically past, a phantom mask on each sail. . . . A little later came *Gitana,* that lovely blue/black ocean racer owned by Lord Rothschild. With her holy-stoned, scrubbed teak deck bleached nearly white by the sun, she bore down on us, her lee-rail just awash and her crew poised on the deck, handling the sheets, as if in a scene from *Swan Lake.*

And now for Toulon and the first sailing trials of *Club Méditerranée.* When you step aboard this 230-foot-long racing machine, for a second or two you do not appreciate its full size, as the wheelhouse and flying bridge break the long sweep of the deck from bow to stern. On this occasion sails, sheets, blocks, tools, sailmakers, welders, painters, food, wine bottles—everything was on deck in glorious confusion.

72-odd metres long, with a waterline length of 66½ metres, four masts, four mains, four large jibs, a total sail area of 1,000 square metres, and all sheets being led to a cluster of 36 winches—it seems incomprehensible that all this was to be under the control of one man in the single-handed transatlantic race, Frenchman Alain Colas.

As we moved out in a light air, we had the feel of a big ship. We cruised at seven knots—later, in a Force 6/7, she recorded 15+ knots (the plus was to remain a secret at that time). Each sail fitted to perfection, a few sheeting arrangements and blocks had to be resited, and with the various craftsmen and technical personnel it was a little difficult to photograph the various sections of the craft.

It was noticeable that the seven-ton rudder, which can be operated by push-button control hydraulically, and also on automatic pilot, shifted hardly at all, the great length of the yacht keeping her on a true and steady course.

The wheelhouse is that of a great ship, perhaps resembling a space-ship with its compasses, radios, closed-circuit television monitoring sails, huge electrical panel, its radar and its banks of digital 'read-outs'. It looks exciting—a little inhuman—with just one spartan human touch, a WC and shower-unit in close company.

Every few seconds our position was clicked out on a clock and tape-recorder—by satellite:

LAT   03777
LON   061563
LAT   037777
LON   061564

The power for all this electrical equipment comes from a huge bank of batteries stored below deck, which in turn are charged by wind power, sea power and 54 panels of solar cells mounted on the wheelhouse which in bright sun at high noon were each giving a reading of 2 amps charging-rate. I repeat, all this is under the control of one man, Frenchman Alain Colas. Below deck, keeping company with the engine and batteries, is a large machine made of springs and pulleys: it is Colas' rehabilitation and re-education machine, to help him totally recover from his accident mentioned earlier. Having done his initial 500 miles, he was about to set off on his 1,500 miles as a condition for entering the race.

Do not be under the impression that this is a 'push-button' yacht. All thirty-six sheeting-winches on the deck, together with the mast-winches for raising the sails, must be 'ground in' by hand. The mast-winches, whilst being reasonably low geared, will take all Colas' strength to raise sail, especially if it blows. I thought myself reasonably fit and tried to raise a mainsail, succeeding in getting it only halfway up the mast. I wish Alain all the best of British (and French) luck . . . and now to Plymouth, 5 June 1976, to photograph this epic race once more. . . .

The Singlehanded Transat: 1976

Driving from the south via Le Havre to Plymouth, I had the feeling of a pilgrimage to Mecca. From all over France, dedicated sailing men were converging on England, heading for Plymouth to see their thirty-two representatives sail single-handed to Newport, USA. On arriving, we were greeted by the glorious sight of the 125 final competitors filling the three docks—seventeen different nations. In bright sun, national flags flying and dressed overall, their decks alive with last-minute furious activity—television interviews, photographs, both professional and amateur, journalists—the armada was preparing to sail.

A tiny 'C' class Italian catamaran, *Spirit of Surprise*, just eight metres long, was positioned alongside and gave a sense of incongruity to the scene. The mind boggles at the courage and determination—and discomfort—that *this* man must have to face up to the absolute minimum of four weeks needed to conquer the Atlantic.

The 'armchair critics' were nodding and shaking their heads at *Club Méditerranée*, for inevitably the world's Press were concentrating on her, that being the journalistic way. But it is all the other entrants with the same determination and one hundred times the discomfort that really deserve the publicity. There was the usual questioning as to whether a race of that size should be held at all. I am quite sure that the race should be held. After all Britain and the sea are still free. All that is needed are good seamanship, and the rules and regulations that must be adhered to—and it is here that the organisers must have their 'fingers well pulled out' for the next Transat.

However, we hopped into the helicopter and circled above the start.

Spirit of America, with *Club Méditeranée* in the background

173

Club Med looked like an old mother-hen, with 124 of her chicks scampering about her. Flying down to mast-height fifteen minutes after the start, I could see Alain Colas calmly sitting back eating a plate of Boeuf Bourgignonne, probably cooked by solar energy (or satellite?). There was no bottle of Château Latour in evidence.

Hanging out of a helicopter, with two cameras working fast (for time is money in a hired helicopter), you have little time to appreciate the scene; but I remember the catamarans and trimarans were moving quickly against the bigger craft in the light airs. We flipped back to the airport and waited until two o'clock before going out again to seek out the leaders. The fleet had split up quite well by this time. With an increase in wind *Pen Duick* was well ahead, followed by the trimarans *Spirit of America* and *Three Cheers* and the big catamaran *Kriter* (ex *British Oxygen*). My Number Two son, Kenneth, had trailed the *Boston Whaler* to Plymouth and could be seen flitting from boat to boat securing his photos from sea level.

On returning to land I noticed a sheet of paper being passed from hand to hand: it was a list of the odds on the race from William Hill, the bookmakers, on the day of the race:

Club Méditerranée	5 to 2
ITT (Ex *Vendredi XIII*)	5 to 1
Pen Duick	5 to 1
Kriter	8 to 1
Spirit of America	10 to 1
Wild Rocket	12 to 1
16 to 1 Bar	

We would see the answer in two to three weeks. My bet was on Tabarly. If only I had had the courage to put £100 on him.

The calms turned to storms; in mid-Atlantic high winds and seas struck: M. Fauconnier in *ITT* (Ex *Vendredi XIII*) has a suspected broken arm and has had to retire; the trimaran *Toria*, skippered by Tony Bullimore, has caught fire and turned upside down, the skipper remarkably being rescued by a passing freighter; *Kriter*, the big 'cat', (ex *British Oxygen*), has broken her self-steering gear and cannot be amongst the leaders; Alain Colas has reported high seas and winds and the loss of his foremost jib boom over the side—no easy task for one man in a tempest to hack it free and stop it smashing into the hull: he can only operate now on three masts—not enough to win, I think.

Pen Duick, with the ace 'Tabarly' aboard, is keeping quiet on his radio—not a bleep out of the old fox, so he is probably leading; also no word from Mike Kane in the tri *Spirit of America* or from English Mike McCullen in the tri *Three Cheers*. It is now 15 June, and I cannot but admire the guts and tenacity of every one of these seamen in this violent weather. On 18 June, fourteen days out, a report comes in: *Gauloise*, the fifty-seven-footer, has sunk, Pierre Fehlmann miraculously being rescued; *Wild Rival*, sailed by Geoffrey Hales, has done a 360 degree capsize, shaken herself, and is carrying on; Alain Colas in *Club Med* has hove to for hours repairing most of his sails off Nova Scotia and is now down to sixty-five per cent of his efficiency. We hear an incredible story of *Gulf Steamer* the sixty-foot-long American tri—on her way to England to compete in the Transat she had pitch-poled in a storm and remained upside down after being hit by a 45-foot wave. In hectic seconds Phil Weld and Bill Stevans found themselves standing on the deckhead of the main cabin. She was floating upside down, supported by the air in her aft cabin and the foam construction of her hull and wings. Cutting a hatch open in the glass hull they were able to sit atop the hull and prepare the boat and themselves for what could be a long-awaited rescue. Fortunately they were in the main shipping-lanes between USA and England; five days later they were picked up by a freighter bound for the States. . . . I applaud their cool good judgement and efficient procedure for survival (touched with the hand of Providence) which brought its own reward. It does once more bring up the question of multihulls versus monohulls in ocean crossings: perhaps comparing this capsize with Angus Primrose's (see later) supplies the answer to this question.

There has been a lot of discussion recently about the future of the single-handed transatlantic race. It was intended to be a race to prove the design of yachts, and of course to prove the worth of the sailor, both in the art of racing and navigation. The race itself (with nearly 150 entries in 1976) cuts directly across busy shipping-lanes both inshore and in mid-Atlantic. At night, or when the navigator has earned four hours sleep below, hazards are bound to occur; and with the era of self-steering apparatus, where the yacht can be left to itself on course for hours the tendency for another hour's sleep must be great.

The big ships of the world are most often on automatic pilot in the Atlantic, the man in the crow's-nest now being a thing of the past; and, although a good look-out is the order of the day, at night a tiny yacht even 72 metres long is but a dot on the radar screen. Of course, one yacht can run down another yacht, especially if the two single-handed sailors are asleep down below: as one trimaran sailor said to me, 'I've no desire to be cut into twelve pieces by another single-handed trimaran, especially when I'm asleep.' Yachts have disappeared in the night before now without trace. Tabarly hit a coaster while he was down below during the 1972 race; and more recently Chay Blyth was hit by a German coaster and capsized in his new trimaran *Great Britain* while on his 500-mile trial. I wonder if it is not possible for some sort of radio-signal to be emitted by the yachts, perhaps with a radius of 5 miles, continuously for the duration of the race. This could take the place of the radar reflector and would use only a very small amount of current.

Now we move to the arrival of the racers at Rhode Island. We took the jet from London Airport (with the 278 other passengers—it is well named an 'air bus'). Kenneth and I stuck labels saying *Coke*, *Hamburgers*, and so on on the camera-cases, so as not to attract the attention of passing thieves. It was twelve years since I had last flown to the States. The procedure was still the same—squeals from the younger passengers as they fill in their disembarkation-forms, writing 'Yes, please' as usual in the square marked 'SEX'. One change I noted on the customs-form declaration: 'Are you carrying any live organisms on your person?'—Well, I hope not.

Arriving over New York we saw the skyscrapers screwed down into the city. Still no news of any arrival at Rhode Island, but news of coastal fog, thick, all down that coast—an added hazard. Having hired a sedan (almost as long as a football pitch), we drove to Newport, R.I. The harbour was already stacked with square-rigged ships and a thousand other great yachts preparing for a great rally to New York.

On 29 June, that old fox Eric Tabarly steals into harbour at 03.00 hours, the winner of the Transat single-handed—tired, bearded, but triumphant. Four days out from Plymouth, his self-steering gear was smashed beyond repair in a storm. He thought of retiring, but after resting decided to carry on, steering by hand and occasionally lashing the tiller. For his last four days he has had no sleep with the ever-changing winds, and he has virtually steered his 75-foot *Pen Duick* for nearly twenty days, an incredible feat of endurance through two weeks of storms, at least one Force 10, and 70-knot winds and 40-foot waves. He has been awarded the Legion d'Honneur by his country, France, and I salute him.

Seventeen hours later Alain Colas limps into harbour, having been delayed off Newfoundland to repair equipment; and then, suddenly, seven hours later a tiny 32-foot trimaran *The Third Turtle*, sailed by Canadian Michel Birch, sails into New England—just twenty-four hours behind Tabarly and seven hours after Colas, the third to arrive through storm and strife. The crowds could not believe their eyes when they saw this tiny craft slide into their harbour.

News then starts to arrive. *Spirit of America*, the 70-foot trimaran, was returning to England, having experienced four days of storm with winds exceeding 60 knots.

'The sheets on the heavy weather sails snapped and the slides on the mainsail tore out at the same time. The life-raft tore free and was washed overboard together with the safety netting between the hulls. The sheets and slides were replaced, but the next day was worse: the waves smashed a 3′ × 1′ hole in the underside of the crossbeam and we started to ship water fast.'

On his way back, Mike Kane said he covered 300 miles in one day, and several days covered 250 miles.

Angus Primrose, in his stock 33-foot monohull *Demon Demo*, experienced a 360-degree capsize when 1,000 miles out from Plymouth.

'In high winds and a very confused sea, with the wind reaching 70 mph, I was just about to come out on deck when the hull took a violent roll—everything went dark and tons of water came into the cabin—in about five seconds (which no doubt seemed like five hours) it was again light, with papers, charts, cooking-stove and sandwiches awash in the cabin below. Going on deck, the mast was over the side, so I had to release the rigging screws to save the mast from smashing the hull. For the rest of the storm, the hull behaved perfectly and the next day I fitted a jury rig with the spi pole and the jib and storm main. The steering vane had also gone over the side, but as I had a spare I replaced it. How the hell can you estimate the strength of mast necessary to withstand conditions like that?'

He took three weeks to sail back to Plymouth under this jury rig.

Yann Nedellec, the young Frenchman in *Objectif Sud II* capsized 360 degrees three times. During the third capsize he smashed his vertebrae. Notwithstanding, he rigged a jury rig and sailed a thousand miles back— the doctors marvel how he ever lived.

I like Mike Richey's signal from *Jester*—a little boat just twenty-six feet long which had been across the Atlantic seven times. 500 miles out, in violent storms, he sent: 'Retiring in favour of a cruise round Ireland.' A wise man!

Regrettably there was no news of Mike McCullen in *Three Cheers*. He had intended to take the northerly route across, but this route had particularly bad weather, and he was presumed lost. How fate sometimes strikes so terribly in a family, for his wife lost her life only days before the race, in an unfortunate accident working aboard *Three Cheers*.

I give a grand salute to Clare Francis—a mere slip of an English girl who battled her way across the Atlantic, weathering all the storm and strife in her tiny *Robertson's Golly*. She should be given an Olympic Gold.

Operation Sail: New York

It's 1976, and come hell or high water the American nation are going to celebrate their 200th year of independence on the Fourth of July. To help them celebrate, ships from almost every nation in the world have been asked to attend a rally of Tall Ships at Newport, Rhode Island, to sail down to New York and then up the Hudson River past Manhattan. These Tall Ships and many many others have sailed to Tenerife, thence to Bermuda, and onward to Newport for this final event.

On 1 July the harbour at Newport was a forest of spars, of yards, of flags from every conceivable nation. The morning dawned with thick fog— apparently a normal happening in this area at this time of the year—but by ten o'clock the hot sun and wind started to burn it off and we went afloat in our small 17-foot launch—small, to enable us to manoeuvre quickly and accurately between the other 2,999 craft that suddenly seemed to be around us. The two fine schooners *Bill of Rights* and the *America* were already sailing their elegant way through the harbour. At twelve o'clock precisely, the American coastguard Tall Ship *Eagle* set sail and led the cavalcade out of Newport Harbour, followed by the full-rigged ship *Amerigo Vespucci* from Italy, and then by *Christian Radich*, *Danmark*, *Dar Pomorza*, the mighty 371-foot barquentine *Esmeralda* from Chile, the 350- foot topsail-schooner *Juan Sebastian de Elcano* from Spain, and the four- masted Russian barque *Kruzenshtern*, all 375 feet of her. Next came the *Libertad* from Argentina, the Japanese barque (318 feet) *Nippon Maru*, the *Gorch Fock* from Germany, the *Sagres* from Portugal, the *Mircea* from Rumania and the *Tovarisch* from Russia. My cup was full, and in our cockleshell of a launch we needed eyes in the back of our heads to

Esmeralda, in New York

manoeuvre and obtain clear and unobstructed views of these ships. The coastguards had had the brilliant idea of having a fire-float on each side of the procession, with a huge jet of water to keep the multitude away from the ships. This wasn't good for the salt-water-conscious cameras, and we cursed the coastguards—but only gently, as their precautions eventually enabled us to get an uncluttered view of these magnificent ships.

The Tall Ships were followed by two hundred other sailing ships representing the naval and maritime history of the world, a feast for any person with a drop of sea-water in his veins. We had decided that if the wind was fresh the next day, we should charter a small aircraft and fly down the coast at about midday to see if we could sight these great ships under full sail. The day broke with a good breeze, and we set our course south. After one hour we sighted the *Eagle* followed by the *Esmeralda*, both under full sail at a speed of 12 knots—an unforgettable sight. We had the impression of being an albatross gently circling those ships far out to sea. Turning west over Long Island Sound, we saw *Club Méditerranée* looking like a slender pencil on the sea with her tight Bermudan rig and 72-metre length in direct contrast to the square-rigged ships; she looked every bit the modern ocean-going yacht.

Returning to Newport after a rewarding day, we dined with our American friends and once again sampled their wonderful hospitality. A favourite dish on the restaurant menu was a huge Maine Lobster and a pound of fillet steak—together: a strange mixture by our standards, but it seemed to be well appreciated.

We then drove back on the highway to New York at the maximum speed allowed, 55 mph (which was an eye opener), across the maze of bridges and tunnels and flyovers, past an amusing sign which said SQUEEZE LEFT, round a bend into the heart of the city. The city is the same as ever, with the exception of the two twin towers of the World Trade Centre, 110 floors high (but the express lift can take you to the 40th floor in seven seconds).

Judging from the papers the next day, coupled with a visit to the headquarters of 'Op Sail', a certain amount of panic seemed to have hit the city. All helicopters had been cancelled through fear of possible air collisions; the number of Press boats were being strictly limited and positioned; and the Press were writing that 'with six million extra people in New York to view the procession, balconies on the flats and houses were bound to crash'. We cancelled our helicopter, but 'our man in New York' had succeeded in getting us our own launch, so we positioned ourselves close under the Statue of Liberty, in order to place the oncoming ships in front of the backdrop of Manhattan Island, and waited for the cavalcade. The first ship to arrive was again the *Eagle,* preceded by a large fire-float spraying three high plumes of water into the air: one red, one white, and the third blue. Only the Americans could think of an idea like that. High above, floating noiselessly in the air, was the dirigible blimp *Good Year*, a nostalgic reminder of the days of the R101 and the *Graf Zeppelin*.

One by one the great ships swept past Manhattan, turning at the top of the river and returning under full sail in their majestic urgency—suddenly to shorten sail, round up, and moor alongside the quays and piers, giving the huge crowds their opportunity to swarm over the decks and marvel at a sight most of them will never see again.

Beken shop, 1975

While in New York, we accepted with pleasure an invitation to lunch at the New York Yacht Club, in the heart of the city. The Club has a model room which contains a model of every challenger and defender of the America's Cup since its inception. They are laid out alongside each other, so that you can take in at a glance the changes of design over the years.

Ranged against these are fine models of other classic world-famous yachts, amongst them those of the famous designer Herreshoff, of whose schooners we have so many fine photographs filed for posterity. The America's Cup itself still stands in its place (reputedly bolted through to the floor), and, like the Koh-i-Noor diamond, waits to be lifted. The whole place is an absolute haven of peace in that noisy city. Returning to England once more, I was grateful to have had the chance to experience again yet another facet of the ever-changing aspects of the sea, which has always been a necessary and enjoyable part of my life.

A little later in 1976 it was the turn of the one-tonners to race at Marseilles. These one-tonners have the reputation of being the 'hot shots' of ocean racing and, although built to a restricted formula, they give plenty of scope to their designers. For one of the races—against my better judgement—I went out to photograph with two photo-journalists and a driver. It was a classic example of how two or more photographers cannot seriously photograph from the same boat, if only for the same reason that each has a different idea of where he wants to go. The boat was in effect a fast launch, about five metres long with a cockpit about two metres square (with four people on board!) There must have been enough expensive camera equipment aboard to have bought a small oil-rig in the North Sea: my companions were 'machine-gunning' their quarry with Canons (!), their telephoto lenses under my arms, and each was giving the driver different directions. Driving back to harbour, the floor of the launch collapsed, the accelerator and control-lever had to be lashed to the hull with wire, the steering-column was about to fall to pieces, and the safety hand-rails had disintegrated.

I shudder to think of the wives and insurance claims that could have been left behind if that launch had sunk—a launch that had been hired as 'fit to go to sea'. The launch hire-firm should have been thrown into jail. The occasion only confirms once more the necessity of a photographer having his own boat to himself; and that boat, like the fast car, must be in first-class condition, for the photographer's work and reputation are at stake—and very often his life.

Over a period of forty years, the style and presentation of photography have varied, as in the fashion world, according to the demands of the publicity and advertising machine, from the stiff portraiture to the coarse-grained enlargement, from the soft focus to the surrealistic. The original photograph has been cut, cropped and maltreated, to be no longer recognisable by the photographer.

I don't think it would be amiss just here to comment on the camera and the photographer in general. I have been fortunate enough to have been brought up in the world of camera, pyro-soda developer and acid fixer—the smells are with me to this day. Just as I watched closely the building of my first boat, so every would-be young photographer should watch the professionals. I remember one old painter craftsman, having put the final top gloss-enamel coat of paint on a racing yacht, telling me that the next day he would immediately wash the whole of the hull with fresh water—'to seal the paint', he said—so that when the decks were washed down later the dirty water washing through the scuppers would not permanently stain the paint on the hull. So it is with a camera. The young enthusiast should strip down an old stand-camera and study how it works, and how the professional uses it. He should see how the 'rising' front and adjustable back of this camera are used to avoid the tall buildings in the photo falling in towards the centre, a thing so often seen in today's journals where the photographer has simply not bothered to correct. The student should use this camera with a single film-slide that just takes one photo, develop the slide and study it for flaws (too much or too little exposure, sharpness of the focus, depth of focus, etc.) and then go back and take a better photo.

Having mastered these techniques, he can then choose a camera for his job or hobby. The 35mm 'miniature' cameras (which we do not like for our type of work) are well-suited for journalistic reproduction and normal size enlargement. Of course, the greater the enlargement, the greater the grain shows. The Nikons, Canons and Leicas are all excellent, and the completely automatic cameras present 'no strain on the brain'—if that is what you want! They do not, however, *make* a photograph. It is rather like comparing a machine-gunner with a sniper. The trained sniper gets his quarry with one shot. If you have an expensive camera at sea, seal all the joints with plastic masking tape—it doesn't look so good but it is professional. And two more tips are worth knowing: if you are not sure of the exposure, point the exposure meter at the back of your hand and you will obtain an average reading for your exposure; also, always use the fastest speed of your shutter—if God has given you 1/1000th of a second, use it.

While the style of photography may change, the scene never changes. Nowadays, the demand is for action photographs, so let us go over to the Mediterranean again—to where the Mistral has been blowing great guns, Force 8/9 rising to Force 10. Now, the Mistral comes from the Rhone Valley, while pent-up pressures of air explode seaward through the narrow neck of the Alps on the east and the Pyrennees on the west. For action photography at sea, it is fine, since you get bright sun with it. The big ocean racers—*Il Moro de Venezia, Gitana, Helisara*—slip their leash and thrash their way to the first mark, 25 miles to windward. With us, all hell is let loose. We tuck ourselves under their lee quarter; and at 15 knots we are surrounded by spray, followed by sheets of solid bursting water from our bow, followed again by crucifying punishment to our bodies, for with both hands on the camera we have no support. We shoot the crews grinding in their winches, their decks awash with white water, and look aloft to see the towering mast of *Helisara* high above us—if it breaks, well that is another hazard. By four o'clock, about ten miles out, we have had enough—a hard day, bruising and exciting, and the seas for our little boat are mountainous. It is at times like this that you bend down and kiss the engine; it was only three hours later in the same area that the French one-tonner *Ariel* was so tragically lost with all hands.

Round the World Racing

In September 1973, the firm of Whitbread sponsored a race from Portsmouth (England) around the world, with stops at Capetown, Sydney and Rio de Janeiro and return to England. Incredibly, nearly twenty yachts started one sunny afternoon: *Great Britain II*, skippered by Chay Blyth; *Pen Duick VI* with the ace Frenchman Eric Tabarly at the helm; *Burton Cutter*, skippered by Leslie Williams; *Sayula II* with Raymond Carlin as owner and skipper; and a host of others—*Adventure, Export 33, Kriter*, etc—all crewed by tough men.

As we approached the start, the sea was practically covered with escorting craft of every description, and our view from the air was phenomenal. On their way to Cape Town Tabarly lost his mast, sailed to Rio under jury rig, replaced it there, sailed back on course and was later dismasted again—a race that he will remember all his life.

In the Indian Ocean many 'knock-downs' occurred, some turning 360 degrees, and unhappily some crews were lost in the tough punishing gales in this part of the world. When the stories of this 30,000 mile race are told, they will be fascinating. The yachts themselves stood the test, indicating that these designs are the forerunners of the cruising yachts of the future. The winner was *Sayula*, a standard 65 foot Swan glass-fibre hull, designed by Americans Rod and Olin Stephens.

Now we come to 25 August 1977. It is the second round-the-world race. On such an occasion you can crystallise our job in a nutshell (mixed metaphor—sorry!), and the conditions under which we sometimes have to photograph. Our thoughts and apprehensions are of the weather conditions for the race tomorrow, for this is a 'one-off' occasion: if there is rain, fog or a gale, it's a long way to go to Cape Town to get some decent

Chay Blyth's *British Steel*

185

pictures—and we have to have photographs as they will probably be used over the next fifty years in books, studies and reference papers.

Our launch is ready, but we have a helicopter on call just in case. The morning dawns—despair. It is a bad day. At nine o'clock the rain is coming down 'in stair-rods', at ten o'clock it is the same, and again at eleven; so we jump into our helicopter and lift off for the start, which is off Portsmouth at midday. With two minutes to go, the contestants are nosing the line and the crews are sweating at the spinnaker halyards—and it still pours with rain. We photograph the start and then drop down on to the cliffs of the Isle of Wight. Two hours later we lift off again and set course for our quarry. All the boats are under spinnaker, looking glorious, and we circle low over each one to record this special event. *Condor* (GB) is in the lead with a tall, tall mast and a huge yellow spinnaker. I have doubts about that great mast in the Indian Ocean; I think I favour the ketches with their snug rigs, such as *Accutrac*, *Debenhams*, *Disque d'Or* or *Flyer* and the others. It is still raining as we head back to Cowes.

Processing our film, we find the results are satisfactory—more than satisfactory, in fact. I have a theory that the downdraught from the helicopter blades disperses the rain and causes a pocket of clear air through which we photograph. How else can one account for the clear results?—for they are in colour, and colour really needs sun and shade for good results. However, we are content.

On Reflection

The evolution of techniques in motive power, both in the fields of powered craft and sail, have been remarkable. We have come from the 'thump' of the two-stroke petrol/paraffin engine to the gurgle of the modern diesel, from the Egyptian cotton canvas sail to the synthetic Dacron of today. Both tell the story in the sleekness and efficiency of the modern yacht.

The power and might of the ever-changing sea, however, has remained the same. One need only recall the complete destruction of *Morning Cloud* off the south coast in recent years, when this finely-built and strongly-made Class I ocean racer was reduced to matchwood in a southerly gale only a mile offshore. Or think of the 63-foot *Bloodhound*, a product of the drawing-board of Charles Nicholson and built by Camper & Nicholson, which was caught in another southerly gale, in virtually the same area off Selsey Bill, where, with the lee shore rumbling ominously behind them in the night, the crew were forced to drop anchor, abandon ship and leave her to her fate. The gale blew out its fury, and in the morning she was still there, but with pebbles flung back from the beach rolling in her cockpit, still riding at anchor but with every link of her anchor-chain stretched and fused bar-solid.

Then there was the 1979 Fastnet Race, still of recent memory. Organised as always by the most competent of sailors, the Royal Ocean Racing Club, the event had attracted 306 entries. Five days later, 23 yachts sunk or abandoned, 114 crew-members rescued and 15 lost—the worst disaster in ocean racing history.

In light winds at the Saturday start I had photographed them class by class as they gently beat their way westward towards the Channel. On the

Monday they received a midday weather forecast of south-westerly winds, Force 6 to 7. At six o'clock a forecast of Force 8 was issued, confirmed at midnight to be Force 9 to 10. Most of the craft were approaching or in the area of the Fastnet Rock. Suddenly the wind changed to north-westerly, Force 10 to 11, and within half an hour 60-knot winds and 40-foot waves resulted in a badly confused sea—the devil was booted and spurred that night.

The Fastnet tragedy, which affected us all, was seen at dawn on the Tuesday when a huge rescue-team was already on the scene—lifeboats, fishing vessels, helicopters, warships, ocean tugs and tankers. The curtain lifted to reveal abandoned yachts, life-rafts with entire crews aboard, dismasted yachts with their crews harnessed to the safety-rails, crews who had been swept overboard with nothing but their life-jackets—and all this over a wide area of high winds and difficult seas. The courage and heroism of both rescued and rescuers alike was of the highest order: yachts sailed to their friends in distress, helicopter pilots under extreme weather conditions unceasingly lowered their crews into the water to pick up survivors, yacht crews leapt into the great seas in the hope that the helicopters would be able to pick them up quickly enough. . . . The real stories of this episode are yet to be told.

The RORC, which already has stringent rules for the safety of crews and boats (not a single life having been lost in twenty-seven Fastnet Races up to 1979) will have to sharpen their wits even more against the might of the sea. The risk of tragedy seems inseparable from the desire of man to pit his courage and skill against the elements.

In contrast, recall the winter of 1962/3 when the sea froze up in the south of England. The Medina river was frozen over, the boats trapped in a foot of ice. Even sea-birds were frozen to the sea-shore by their feet. An unusual report came from the navigating officer of a Union Castle liner passing Cowes, who reported that he had seen an iceberg in the Solent (probably seen through the bottom of a glass of Martini on the Rocks). . . .

It has been said that Beauty lies in the eye of the beholder. In my search for beauty on the sea I have come to the conclusion, like Uffa Fox, that 'anything which is perfectly designed for its use in the world becomes beautiful'. Just as the arches of fine buildings give great strength, so they give beauty of line. The twin towers of the World Trade Centre on the Manhatten skyline look incongruous in relation to the other buildings, but stand at their base and look upwards—there you will find sheer strength, symmetry and beauty of line. It is the same with a yacht or clipper:

A full-rigged ship, unutterably fair,
Her masts like trees in winter, frosty bright.

Lionheart, 1980 British
contender in the
America's Cup

Of course we have all seen monstrous designs moored in the marinas of the world—huge areas of glass high upon their decks (and therefore impractical to go to sea with), bearing such lovely names as *Sofia*, *Magdalena*, and so on, on their transoms. I term them all *Chez Tomate*. Among these stand out the 'pearls' that make you stop and gaze in wonder; and, although they may belong to the rich, they are there for you to see and enjoy, and not locked up in some vault or other.

I have endeavoured to tell you what my life has been all about, to try and portray the poetry of a yacht and of the sea—the sound of the wind in the rigging and the vicious squalls that knock a yacht on its beam-ends; the terrifying crack and thunderburst of the spinnaker as it whips the air like a wild stallion on the end of a leash. Many people ask, 'What is your most satisfying picture?' and to this I can only quote in reply the words that Imogen Cunningham spoke in her nineties: 'The one we shall take tomorrow.'